CATAPULT

NEW YORK

# Pieces You'll Never Get Back

⚘

A Memoir of Unlikely Survival

Samina Ali

*Pieces You'll Never Get Back*

First Catapult edition: 2025

ISBN: 978-1-64622-261-2

Library of Congress Control Number: 2024947840

*Jacket design by Nicole Caputo*
*Jacket photograph © Rowan Spray / Stills.com*
*Book design by Laura Berry*

Catapult
New York, NY
books.catapult.co

Printed in the United States of America

1  3  5  7  9  10  8  6  4  2

*To my son, Ishmael.*

*And to my daughter, Zaara.*

*My two bookends, holding me sturdy.*


*S.A.*

# Pieces
# You'll Never
# Get Back

# *Prologue*

My son's name is Ishmael.

When I was pregnant and my husband, Scott, and I were researching the name, we discovered its many spellings, depending on the language you speak. *Yishma'el* in the original Hebrew, *Ismael* in Spanish, *Ismaele* in Italian. The French variation changes slightly in pronunciation, *Ismaël*. Those speaking Finnish say *Ismo* while in Persian it's *Esamil*. If you happen to speak Latin, you'd say *Ismahel*. Ukbek and Tajik languages both say *Ismoil* while in Kazakh it's *Smagul*. And in Arabic, my son's name is *Isma'il*. The malleability of the name, its universality, is what drew us to it. While we officially decided on its English spelling, Ishmael, pronounced by his dad and others in the U.S. with two distinct syllables and a long vowel sound stressing the *a*—Ishmāəl—everyone on my side of the family in India, everyone who speaks Urdu, my first language, runs all the letters together into an almost monosyllabic, melodious, and warm *Ismail*.

This is how it was meant to be. His dad and I chose this

name for our son because it perfectly blends his mixed heritage. I was born in India to Muslim parents, grew up both in Hyderabad and across the world, in Minneapolis. Every year until I was nineteen years old, I lived and went to school for several months in the ancient, walled Old City neighborhood of Hyderabad and also lived and went to school for several months in a white suburb of Minneapolis. It's not easy being both a South Indian girl and a Midwestern girl. And I suppose many of my life mistakes came from trying to balance these two identities, like when I agreed at age eighteen to an arranged marriage. Less than two years later, when I filed for divorce, my two brothers told me they found it more surprising that I ever agreed to the arrangement than that I called it quits. The second time around, with Ishmael's dad, I got married the American way, by first falling in love.

Ishmael's father is white—99.9 percent European, according to a DNA test. He grew up in Palo Alto in a family that valued the arts. His mom was a visual artist and his dad a poet and professor of literature. Scott himself earned a graduate degree in English literature from UC Berkeley then went on to earn a second graduate degree, an MFA in poetry writing. That's where we met, in a graduate writing program in the Pacific Northwest, where I was studying to be a novelist. So, the reference to Herman Melville's Ishmael isn't accidental. In *Moby Dick*, Ishmael tells the story of a tyrannical quest for the great white whale that chewed off his captain's leg on a previous voyage. In a state of blind revenge, Captain Ahab risks the lives of his crewmen chasing and battling the whale. At the end of the adventure, only Ishmael and the great whale survive. Of course it's because of this famous literary invitation to "Call me Ishmael" that, one afternoon in a local bookstore, Scott and I stumbled across the name in another book, this one titled something like *What NEVER to Name Your Child!* Finding the name listed there only cemented our decision. Our son was born of two writers, two people who had devoted their lives to the written word, and we hoped to convey the importance of literature through the name. Knowing what I do now about how the act of writing a book would end up saving my life, this decision has taken on an even deeper significance.

There is yet one more book that contributed to my choosing the name Ishmael for my son. Thousands of years ago, long before Prophet Muhammad was born, it was Ishmael who, together with his father, Abraham, built the Ka'ba (cube) in the deserts of Arabia as a house of monotheistic worship. When Muslims make the annual pilgrimage of hajj and circle the Ka'ba, they are commemorating Abraham, who passed an immense test of faith. Although the Qur'an is frustratingly vague about which specific son Abraham was asked to sacrifice, whether it was Isaac, as in the Bible, or if it was actually Ishmael, as Muslim theologians contend, the point of the story is to highlight Abraham's devotion to God. Abraham had long prayed for a son . . . and now God was asking Abraham to sacrifice that very son. Could there be a more difficult test for a prophet? For a father?

When Abraham raises the knife, an angel intervenes. The sacrifice of an animal will suffice. It's a tremendous moment of divine mercy, and each year, millions of pilgrims to hajj slaughter sheep and divide the meat among those in need. It's their way of acknowledging that, even when things are at their bleakest and you've given up all hope, God can still intervene with a miracle.

Some would even say that performing hajj is itself a form of death. The Qur'an repeatedly describes death as a meeting with God and the Ka'ba is the House of God. By traveling to the House of God, pilgrims are shifting away from the material world to the spiritual one. Sins are absolved. Hair is shaved off. Clothes are shed. Replaced by a simple white cloth—just as a newborn body is wrapped after birth, and just as a lifeless body is wrapped and buried Islamically in the ground. Returning from hajj is considered a rebirth and pilgrims are given the title "Hajji" to show that their new, more elevated lives now transcend the petty indulgences of the everyday.

As meaningful as this symbolism eventually turned out to be for me, the grand ideas of pilgrimage and sacrifice and death and rebirth and miraculous grace had little to do with why I initially chose to name my son Ishmael. Back when I was pregnant and confronting the reality of raising a boy, I was inspired by Ishmael's mother, Hagar, and her simple story of faith.

After years of Abraham and Sarah's marriage bearing no children, the King of Egypt gifts Abraham his daughter, Hagar, to bear him a child and heir. Hagar gives birth to Ishmael, but then Sarah herself becomes pregnant. She wants nothing to do with Hagar and her infant son, begotten with her husband. So, Abraham instructs Hagar to pack for a long journey and takes the new mother and their infant son far from Sarah's fury, far from their home in Syria. He leads them into a desolate valley. In the middle of the Arabian desert, Abraham hands Hagar a few dates and a flask of water then turns to leave, cruelly abandoning the two in the scorching landscape.

Before he can get very far, Hagar shouts to Abraham, "Has your Lord instructed you to leave us here alone?"

Abraham confirms that God has indeed willed this seemingly terrible fate.

Hearing this, Hagar boldly answers, "Then God will not abandon us."

Before long, she runs out of water and dates. The air burns her skin. Ishmael starts crying. In desperation, Hagar lays him on the hot sand and races to a nearby hill. She climbs to the top and peers out in the distance. There's nothing except a second hill. No people. No caravan crossing the desert. No distant city. No oasis. Desperate, she begins to run back and forth between the two hills, climbing to the top of one and then the other, her feet sinking deep into the hot sand, her muscles straining. But she doesn't stop. Back and forth she goes, praying, praying, praying for help, two, four, seven times.

The name Ishmael means *God listens*. It's a theophoric name, a name that carries the name of God within it. By bearing a god's name, a person was entrusted to that god for protection. In various ancient Semitic cultures, Ishmael was actually *Yishma'el*. The god carried within Yishma'el is Yahweh. When Hagar was racing from hill to hill, calling out to the heavens for help, she was in fact calling out to Yahweh, to God, to Allah, to the one god her husband, Abraham, had surrendered to, the very god to whom she had entrusted the protection of their child.

God does indeed listen. Angel Gabriel descends. Where Ishmael has been lying alone, striking at the scorching sand with his heels, water miraculously erupts from the dry earth. The holy spring of Zamzam. Mother and child are saved. Hearing of this miraculous spring, nomadic tribes soon gravitate there, creating a city near Zamzam that eventually becomes Mecca.

By naming my son Ishmael, this is the Islam I am anchoring him to, the one that is connected to other faiths by stories and prophets and a shared history and a shared god, and the one that recognizes and honors a woman's courage and a woman's ability to face the elements on her own, even with a child in tow.

Ishmael is a perfect blend of our son's mixed heritage.

A desert Ishmael and the Ishmael of the sea.

# PART ONE

I shall never get you put together entirely,
Pieced, glued, and properly jointed.

—SYLVIA PLATH, "THE COLOSSUS"

*Death*

1

Some part of me knew I was sick right from the start, months before the symptoms appeared.

Not that the symptoms appearing changed anything. Even then, even when the signs were obvious, no one did anything to help me.

2

"Imagine a jigsaw puzzle," my neurologist advised me on the morning of my discharge from the hospital. "Imagine how every single piece must fit together perfectly for that puzzle to make sense. That was your brain before the damage, every piece—every neuron—working in concert with other pieces, a delicate, sophisticated process. Now imagine scattering that puzzle. That's your brain now, little disconnected pieces . . . little islands of neurons within each hemisphere working independently from others. Your job from this day forward is to put back together as many pieces of that puzzle as possible."

3

I have a vivid memory of the anesthesiologist who administered the epidural. By then, my symptoms had exploded, but the doctors and nurses were proceeding as though this were just another routine delivery. It was the attending obstetrician who pushed the epidural on me even when he knew I didn't want it. He thought it would shut me up. He was tired of me complaining that something was wrong. What was it about me that he couldn't stand? Was I just another nagging woman to him? Or worse, was I a brown woman with the audacity to ask a white man to take me seriously? I wasn't complaining about the labor cramps. That pain was nothing compared to the pain in my head and in my chest—parts that have nothing to do with childbirth. He refused to address me. He ordered a nurse to give me Alka-Seltzer. He ordered the anesthesiologist to shoot me up and shut me down.

The anesthesiologist was Indian like me and also around my age of twenty-nine. As she helped ease my huge, laboring body onto its side and bent over me to thrust the longest needle I'd ever seen into my lower back, in the epidural space right outside my spinal cord, she whispered, "I'm sorry. I have no choice."

I was filled with sorrow. The pain in my chest felt like my heart breaking. I'd wanted to be alive to the labor pains, to feel the sensations of my son being born. Once the epidural went in, I expected a band of numbness to encircle my center. But something else happened, something positive for a change. The anesthesiologist knew what she was doing. She purposely angled the needle so that the epidural only numbed one side of my body. The anesthesia split me down the center vertically. The right side of my body went numb while, on the left, I could still feel everything, my left leg down to my toes, every hot, shooting cramp tightening across half my stomach. My enormous belly was the moon, one side in darkness.

Did I thank the anesthesiologist? Dressed in blue scrubs, she wore no makeup and kept her hair pulled back in a tight ponytail at the nape of her neck. After all these years, I can still see her thick eyebrows and the concerned expression on her face.

But when I scrutinize it closely, the memory of her appearance, that tiny piece of the puzzle, is static. She isn't moving or talking. She's absolutely still. And that's how I know my mind is playing a trick on me. What I've stored away is not an actual memory, but a step removed: a memory of the photograph Scott took of her on the day of the delivery. I saw the photograph months later, during that dark era when I was trying my hardest to do what the neurologist had instructed me to do and gather up the puzzle pieces and put them back into place. Even though another part of my brain now understands that this image belongs to a photograph, whenever I think back on my delivery, this static portrait of the doctor still springs forward.

The wrong puzzle piece is bound up in the new wiring of my brain.

4

When my neurologist told me that the damage from the strokes had left my brain broken and scattered, when he declared matter-of-factly in his soft, earnest tones that my recovery depended upon me putting it back together as best I could, that there was nothing more the doctors or medicine could do to heal the damage, what he didn't mention was that some of the pieces were simply gone. The strokes had cut off blood flow and burst open vessels. Brain cells had been killed. Obliterated when particular neurons clustered in a space smaller than a pencil eraser were wiped out, destroyed by the hemorrhaging.

He also didn't tell me that, unlike other organs, the brain can't regenerate neurons, blood vessels, or tissue structures.

This is why, despite suffering from multiple organ failure, my liver and kidneys and lungs were able to switch back on and begin repairing themselves. My blood started clotting again. From a dismal count of seven, my white blood cell count climbed back up into the standard range in the thousands. And my blood pressure gradually dropped down to normal. The body has a miraculous power to heal, and even, in some cases, to regenerate. I wish I didn't know this truth as intimately as I do.

The MRI scans of my brain communicate what my neurologist never did. Since nerve cells don't regenerate, the old damage is right there, visible as iron spots, dark areas in my brain where the cells are no longer functioning. Pieces of me that I will never get back.

# 5

For fifteen years now, I have sat and written this story from beginning to end. As a result of the brain trauma, parts of my life have disappeared. Memories have vanished along with connections to people I once knew and loved. The injury took from me my sense of self, my beliefs and values, my ties to Islam and to India, my love for the written word. When I became pregnant with my son, I hadn't realized that ushering in his life would require me to give up my own.

How can you make sense of your life when pieces of it are missing? The word *memoir* means an account of the author's personal remembrances. But I don't have first-hand memories of the most life-changing event I've endured. And the two snippets of memory I do have of the five days I was in a coma are so haunting that I lack the wherewithal to explain what it is I'm remembering.

So, as I sit at my desk once more to try to write this story, I find myself taking a cue from my own brain. Similar to how new neural connections were forced to forge pathways around darkened clusters of dead brain cells, my narrative seems only to work when I connect it to others' to get around those holes in my memory and understanding: stories Scott and my parents told me about how they endured those days I was unconscious, the story I've been able to discern of my sickness from my thick medical files, and even those larger stories I grew up hearing about what it means for me to be a good Muslim girl who ends up in paradise. Now that I've been at death's door, how will I explain those same allegories about angels and the hereafter and heaven and hell to my own son? I have threaded my personal narrative through these others, and, in this way, I've tried to bring these irretrievable parts of me back into existence, hoping to make myself whole again.

# 6

Over the years, whenever I've described what happened to me, I've said that my pregnancy first presented like a textbook example of a healthy, normal pregnancy. Then, quite unexpectedly, during the third trimester, I began experiencing strange symptoms that gradually escalated over those final five weeks until there was no denying that something had gone terribly wrong.

But that's not what happened. It's just the story I tell people because the truth is too complicated to explain.

The disorder that infected my pregnancy originated with the pregnancy itself. Approximately five or six days after fertilization, a ball of cells called a blastocyst travels down into the uterus, where it attaches to the uterine wall. The moment the blastocyst attaches is called implantation— and my implantation didn't go correctly.

When nothing goes right in a pregnancy, a woman will miscarry. A pregnancy is, after all, a complicated process where thousands of maternal and embryonic and fetal cells change. It's a remarkable feat of biological engineering and, in my case, most everything in the machinery of those cellular structures and processes was actually running smoothly, which was the reason my pregnancy limped forward. The only kink was the improper implantation. And that one tiny error kicked off a series of developments deep in my body, the start of what would culminate in the almost complete disintegration of my vascular and nervous systems.

It took over seven months for the first warning signs to appear. But back when I first took the early detection test two or three weeks after implantation and gleefully discovered I was pregnant, the baby and I were already in danger.

7

I knew from the start that something was wrong with my pregnancy.

And, from the very start, I began pestering my obstetricians. Scott taught at Stanford at the time, and I was under the care of some of the best medical professionals in the country at what was then UCSF-Stanford Hospital. At a routine exam early in my first trimester, one of the residents wheeled a sonogram machine into the exam room and hooked me up and happily pointed to a small smudge on the screen. As round and tiny as a Cheerio. That was my baby, she told me, exactly where he ought to be. Then she turned up the volume on the machine until the strength of my son's galloping heartbeat overwhelmed me with relief, and I could do nothing more than look up at the resident with tears in my eyes and thank her for going out of her way to reassure me.

On my way home, the nagging feeling that something wasn't right started up again.

# 8

The best way to imagine memory loss is to think of what it's like when you look at a picture of yourself as a baby. Your parents tell you that the person in the picture is you. They tell you what you were like, whether you were a colicky baby, whether you were happy and bubbly. You know for a fact that for those first four or five years of your life, you ate dinner every night, that you played with your toys, that you began toddling then walking then running, that you learned to speak by first learning colors and numbers and shapes, by listening to and then imitating your parents. Yet you have no memory of any of this. Having no memory doesn't mean these events didn't occur. All those moments exist, just not inside you.

Most of what I know about what actually happened during my delivery is from other people: Scott, my mom, my best friend, Naomi, the attending obstetrician, and the chief resident—although neither the attending nor the chief resident spoke to me, not when I was delivering my son in the luxurious penthouse suite on the fifteenth floor of the hospital and especially not afterward when I landed in a grim, windowless space in the neuro-ICU, my brain lit up by its own demise. I only know the doctors' perspectives from their notes in my medical file.

I also have photographs of the events as they were unfolding. Like any first-time dad, Scott was eagerly snapping away, documenting the arrival of his son. The delivery suite had a lounge area with a sofa and plush armchairs, and a large TV fastened high on a wall. In one of the photos, my mother and older brother are sitting side by side on the sofa. ("What was my brother doing in the delivery room?" I say to Scott when I later see the photo. I'm scandalized. "Did he see me naked?" "Your legs weren't stretched out in stirrups for the entire labor," Scott teases me. "Don't worry. Your brother left when it was time for the delivery." "I didn't know my mom was there. I thought she flew in after the birth." "Your dad flew in after. She came in a week before to help out." "And Naomi? When did she arrive?")

So, what have I recovered? Or, as my neurologist asked me on several occasions, the first being right after I woke up from a coma in the neuro-ICU: What is the last thing I remember?

I remember the pain. I'm not talking about the pain of labor. The pain I remember—the pain I will never forget—was the pain in my head. I'd never felt such debilitating pain before. I couldn't keep my eyes open. And when the nurse demanded that I open them and push the baby out, I noticed I was seeing double, and then triple. The pain was at the very core of my head, meaty and defined, like an animal nesting in the spongy ridges of my brain.

"Help me," I remember saying. My legs were up in stirrups. So the pain must have started in the second stage of labor, while I was pushing. I remember trying to get the obstetrician's attention. He was not a doctor I'd consulted during my pregnancy, but someone who happened to be on call the night I was in labor. I remember him refusing to look at me, intent on guiding the resident, a young woman named Gillian who sat on a stool between my legs. I remember Scott being confused and asking the doctor if he'd heard me complaining about my head and chest, then repeating my wish for pain medication. I remember the obstetrician barking at Scott in his Australian accent: "Your wife is being dramatic!" I remember wondering why the resident, a woman herself, was following the doctor's lead, refusing to help me, to look at me even. I was giving birth at a prestigious hospital in San Francisco, yet these doctors refused to hide their contempt for me. They broadcast their intolerance loud and clear through the birthing room. They only spoke to the nurses, who in turn spoke to me.

Even through the pain, I knew what was happening. I grew up in America. It didn't matter that my family was wealthy or that I was educated or even that my husband was white. Nothing leveled the playing field. I am a brown woman. And these two white doctors felt it beneath them to help a brown woman deliver her baby. They could barely stand to touch me . . . even with their hospital gloves on.

That's one piece of the puzzle, one shard.

# 9

When the anesthesiologist visited me in the neuro-ICU, she told me that neither the OB with the Australian accent nor his chief resident were allowed to see me or my family. The hospital was scared of a lawsuit. They'd put the two doctors on leave. What went down during delivery shouldn't have gone down that way, she said, and she would be willing to testify, if I wanted to take that route. I had her full support if I wanted to go down that path. She said all this in hushed tones, looking about to make sure no one heard her.

She was telling me something important. I sensed this through the brain trauma. But I couldn't grasp what it was. I had no memory of her. No memory of the delivery. I didn't even know that I was in a hospital.

What mistakes was she talking about?

What baby?

## 10

When I walked into the elevator on the ground floor of the hospital, my contractions fifteen minutes apart, a hot band tightening around my center until I couldn't breathe, I was overcome with an uncontrollable urge to remove the baby from my body, along with my belly, set it all on the ground of the elevator and step back off by myself, to get as far away as possible. Some part of me knew I wouldn't make it out of the delivery room, and I wanted nothing to do with my son. I remember digging my fingernails into my sides, trying to pry off my own belly. My eyes filled with tears. When the elevator doors closed and Scott pressed the button for the top floor, I thought, *This is it. This is the end.*

On the long ride up to the fifteenth floor, Scott must have spoken encouraging words to me. He must have kept his arm around my waist, supporting me during the worst of the contractions. With his other hand, he must have been carrying the overnight bag, which I'd packed weeks before with the clothes I'd planned for my newborn and me to wear home from the hospital after the delivery. People must have been crammed into that elevator around us, as there always were— doctors and nurses, orderlies, visitors, getting on, stepping off—on almost every floor. A few must have smiled at Scott, congratulating him. They didn't understand what was happening, of course. They thought that I was just another pregnant woman about to have her baby. That this was a happy occasion.

At some point, an orderly pushed an empty wheelchair onto the elevator, on his way to relaying it to a patient in need, but instead, in watching me grip the steel rod running along the interior wall of the elevator and slump forward in pain, he pushed the wheelchair against the backs of my legs, urging me to sit. I felt the hard leather of the seat pressing my calves, the sensation of it against my body annoying me, but I had to grit my teeth and wait for the contraction to pass before I was able to wave him away. It's all there, in the fragmented memories I've been able to recover, moments unconnected to others, neurons floating in isolation on islands—but doesn't that alone, the fact that these are recovered memories, make them suspect?

As the elevator rose, so too did my anxiety. Slowly, gradually, floor by floor, I became increasingly agitated. I dug my fingers as far as they would go into my belly. More people got on, others got off. Scott was murmuring in my ear. The orderly was again urging me to sit in the wheelchair. A man shook Scott's hand. We had almost reached the maternity ward. There was no turning back. And right then, just when I felt I would burst open from the strain, my brain suddenly switched off. Everything went quiet. My arms went limp by my side. I stared blankly at the round buttons across the top of the elevator doors, announcing each successive floor. The activity around me became a blur. What was the use in resisting? We were climbing up. The minutes were counting down. I had no choice but to accept my grim reality. The baby was coming.

## 11

The OB with the Aussie accent wasn't the first doctor to dismiss me. He just happens to be the easiest one for me to blame. He was trapped in that delivery room with me for fourteen hours. He insisted on treating the delivery like it was routine even when it became clear there was nothing routine about it. And yet, during the nine months of my pregnancy, how many OBs had I sought out for help in that prestigious practice and how many maintained, in spite of my protests, that everything was routine?

I was twenty-nine years old. I was healthy and fit. I had no underlying conditions. I was happily married to my college sweetheart. We were eager to start a family. I can see how my life read to them from the outside.

The truth was something very different. I arrived at the hospital to have a baby. And I left disabled.

# 12

"Help me," I remember saying to the attending OB.

Then Scott repeating my words to the doctor. "She's asking for help . . . excuse me, Doctor, she's saying she wants you to help her."

I remember how difficult it was becoming to breathe. I remember asking why my head and chest felt like they were about to burst open. "Shouldn't I be hurting down there? Why am I hurting up here?" The nurse repeated my questions to the attending. He ordered her to administer Alka-Seltzer. I remember barfing it back up on her white canvas shoes.

Now the left side of my body, the side not drugged by the epidural, also went numb. The animal in my head burrowed deeper in its nest. I passed out. I was awoken by the nurse, reminded to push. Each time I pushed, the pressure intensified inside my skull, the animal grew more ferocious. I began seeing double. Then triple. The T-waves of my heart lines inverted. My blood pressure, which at the start of my pregnancy had been 80/60, rose to 130/70 then rose again to

140/90 then rose even higher to hover in the 180s/100s. My systems were erupting.

"Pain," I remember saying to Scott. "So much pain." My words were slurring.

"The doctor won't talk to me. I've tried several times."

"Get the resident . . . woman."

"She won't talk to me either. Why do you have one eye closed?"

"Two of you . . ."

I didn't have the strength to speak. Each time I passed out, I remember being shaken awake by the nurse, ordered to push. Each time I was shaken awake, I had to work to remember where I was, what I was in the middle of doing. Why did I have to push? Each time I pushed, the pressure aggravated the meaty pain at the core of my head and I passed out.

"The baby is in distress," Scott told me, standing at my side. There was meconium. There was chorioamnionitis. There was fetal tachycardia with repetitive deep variable decelerations. They had to get him out right away. I wasn't making as much progress as they'd wanted with my pushing. And I'd been pushing for four hours. Four hours! The attending was going to chalk this up to maternal exhaustion. He'd decided to use forceps. He had to cut me. The nurse offered nitrous oxide to numb the pain. I snatched the mask and stuck it over my face and sucked in the gas. Fuck the labor! I needed to numb my head and chest. I remember I could actually feel the gas floating up into my skull like a thick layer of fog blowing in off the ocean. I could feel the gas hanging thickly over my brain. Something told me it was making matters worse, but I grabbed at the mask over and again.

The nurse snatched my attention. "A contraction is coming!" she shouted.

I couldn't feel it. My head was a boulder. The pain in my chest made it impossible to breathe.

"Push on three," she ordered. "One, two . . ."

I did as I was told.

"Once again," she yelled.

I vomited on my chest. Another nurse cleaned me off. I pushed harder. "He's almost out," said a voice. I felt my son's body, long and lean, slide out of me. I remember the relief. I remember the nurse holding him up for me to see. I remember staring at him with one eye closed tight. I remember being shocked by how fair he was. I had imagined he'd be brown, like me. I'd spent months warning his white dad to educate himself on what it would mean for him to have a brown baby. I hadn't expected that my son would be paler than his father, that he'd have gray-blue eyes and blond hair. How did that come out of me? Then I remember being shaken awake. Had I fallen asleep? My son was being weighed in the corner. Scott was taking photos. The consulting cardiologist, a doctor I hadn't seen before, had materialized next to me. My blood pressure was 240/160.

"How many fingers am I holding up?"

I struggled to speak. "Two." My head felt like it was about to crack and this amphibian, this animal that had made a nest of my brain, would finally crawl out. Something else had just come out of me. What was it, another animal? I couldn't remember. "See five, six of each."

"Now how many?"

What did it matter? All my strength was gone. I couldn't speak. And that's when it happened, right when the cardiologist held up his fingers to my face, that's when my memory diverges from everyone else's.

In my medical file, the doctors wrote that during the cardiologist's examination, I had a grand mal seizure, the most severe type of seizure a person can have, which cut off oxygen to my brain for thirty seconds. The chest pains the doctor had dismissed with Alka-Seltzer had been a heart attack. The head pain the doctor had insisted was me being dramatic, forcing me to try to push my baby out for four hours when the standard length for the pushing stage is no more than two, was the result of ischemia, the cascade of minor strokes. At the front of my head, on the right side, I had also suffered a potentially lethal subarachnoid hemorrhage. My blood platelet count was crashing to dangerous levels. Fluid was filling my lungs and brain and flesh. My organs began shutting down.

Ishmael was being weighed and bathed. Scott recalls he was in the middle of taking photos of our newborn when he heard a shout to clear the room. Commotion ensued. More shouts. A clattering of something metal hitting the floor. He turned to see my legs and my arms thrown up in the air, stiff as logs, and my entire body convulsing. The violence of the sight rooted him to the spot. A male nurse tackled Scott backward out the door. Another nurse grabbed my son and frantically wrapped him in a blanket and rushed him to the nursery.

The door to the penthouse delivery suite slammed shut behind my husband and my newborn son, locking them both out. Several medical staff threw their weight on me and held me down and injected me with magnesium sulfate.

I fell into a coma.

•

## 13

"It's sad when a patient feels her concerns are being dismissed," one of the OBs told me during one of my routine visits. It was late in the pregnancy. Four weeks from my due date. I was enormous. My feet didn't fit into my shoes. My wedding ring didn't slide on. When I worked on my novel, my fingers were so bloated that when I typed I would feel them rubbing up against each other. I didn't recognize my face in the mirror. I was a puffer fish under attack. I was a helium balloon. I was the full moon. For minutes on end, I would stick a finger into my cheek to see how deep it would sink into my flesh.

"I don't feel right," I said. "I have headaches. I'm seeing specks. Look at how bloated I am! And I'm itching all over. I've got fingernail marks all over me. Look!"

I watched her page through my chart, carefully reading the shorthand entries the various obstetricians had penned at each of my visits over the past several weeks.

Headaches? It wasn't unusual for some women to endure migraines late in pregnancy, even those women, like me, who didn't have a history. Migraines can be accompanied with vision changes, such as floating specs.

Bloating and puffiness? There were plenty of causes: heat, water retention, weight gain, gas, constipation, even the pregnancy hormones themselves. Swelling is one of the most common complaints of pregnancy. Just drink more water in order to flush my body of excess fluids, they told me.

Reduced urine output? Dehydration from vomiting.

Vomiting? A result of the baby pushing up against my stomach.

The abdominal pain on my right side? Several thick ligaments surround and support the womb while it grows during pregnancy. As the uterus expands, the ligaments stretch. Because the pain was on the right side, it was likely the round ligament causing the issue, strained by any number of reasons: coughing, sneezing, rolling over in bed, laughing, even my recent jump in weight—which itself was normal in the final weeks of pregnancy as the fetus grew an impressive half a pound a week. I was advised to take Tylenol for relief.

"And what about the itching?" I asked. It was now two weeks from delivery, and my condition was getting worse. Why couldn't the doctors see that? I was lying on a hospital bed in the OB triage, which served as the pregnant patients' ER. I was scratching my thighs as I spoke, my fingernails leaving long red trails up and down my skin. My headaches had intensified. I couldn't keep anything down, not even water. I was hooked up to an IV. Scott was rushing up I-280 from Stanford. He'd cut his classes short. He apologized for not taking this more seriously. He didn't know what to think, he told me, because the doctors kept insisting that I was fine. But now he was as alarmed as me.

"Pregnancy can be miserable," the OB was telling me, "especially this late into it." She pulled a stool next to my cot and gently placed her hand over mine and squeezed, stopping me from scratching. "Feeling like something isn't going right can suddenly add a tremendous amount of stress. But I can assure you," she said, "that your generalized symptoms aren't what we consider to be in the red zone. Would you like me to prescribe a lotion for the itching?"

"A lotion won't help," Scott said to the male OB. It was now the day before I delivered, and Scott had come with me to what turned out to be my last clinic visit. Since my stay in OB triage, we'd been paging through the book *What to Expect When You're Expecting*. We thought we knew what was wrong with me. We thought we'd diagnosed this ourselves. We thought it would be better if Scott spoke directly to the obstetrician, sure we'd be taken more seriously if it came from a white man.

"We think this is cholestasis," Scott told the OB.

"Cholestasis?" the OB repeated.

Scott glanced at me. The doctor sounded incredulous. And we hadn't yet finished saying what we'd come to say. "Yes, cholestasis. We want you to run blood tests and make sure her liver is okay."

"You want me to run a blood test for cholestasis?"

This wasn't going the way we'd hoped. In the small exam room, I was sitting next to Scott on a matching plastic chair. The OB sat across from us, my file open on his lap. He was scribbling something into my file. I reached over and squeezed Scott's hand, encouraging him to say the rest of what we'd planned. He cleared his throat. The doctor looked up at him. He could tell from Scott's face that there was more we had to say. He put his pen down.

"Some of her symptoms also sound like preeclampsia," Scott blurted out. It was hard for him to say this because it was hard for us to believe. We didn't want it to be true. Preeclampsia is a serious disease, a fatal disease. The most common disease of pregnancy. Yet I couldn't deny the relief I felt now that the name of the disease had been spoken out loud. First-time moms tend to go beyond their due date by two weeks. There was still time to treat this. "Is there a test you can run," Scott was pressing the doctor, "to check? We're a little nervous."

"What do you do for work?" the OB asked Scott. In my medical chart, in the area for notes on this visit, he scribbled that Scott taught writing and critical thinking full-time at Stanford. That he'd earned a graduate degree in English literature from Berkeley and then a second masters in poetry. Then he asked what I did for a living, jotted down that I was working on my first novel. It didn't take long for Scott and me to understand what the doctor was doing. He was putting us in our place, making sure Scott and I understood how absurd it was for us, two writers with no medical background, to question him, a specialist at a top-ranked hospital.

I didn't have the neurologist's analogy of the broken puzzle to help me back then. I didn't know that the OBs were looking at each symptom individually, that not one of them had thought to put all the pieces together.

That very night, just hours after the prenatal visit, I went into labor.

## 14

The first time I heard the doctors diagnose me was after I woke up from the coma. Even then, the news didn't come from an OB, but from my neurologist. After months of begging, a doctor was finally identifying the disease, but I was too debilitated to understand what he was saying. The brain damage was so extensive that it even kept me from grasping that anything was wrong with me.

## 15

It took four years of rehabilitation before I was well enough
to return to the question I had asked during my delivery.
Why were organs that had nothing to do with pregnancy and
childbirth damaged?

I requested a copy of my medical files covering the period I was in the neuro-ICU. I had no memory that I'd suffered twenty-one medical conditions, requiring that I be
under the care of nine different specialists: obstetrics and
gynecology, pulmonary, renal, hematology, cardiology, in-
fectious disease, hepatology, gastroenterology, and of course
neurology. When the files arrived by mail to my house, accounting for just five days and nights yet so thick they had
to be stuffed inside several manila envelopes, I should have
known that the answer I was desperately searching for would
continue to elude me. But I proceeded to stack the pages
chronologically—a pile on my dining table that rose almost
three inches high. There were doctors' handwritten notes
from every visit, lengthy blood test reports from ongoing

blood draws, summarized findings from X-rays and MRIs of my brain, results from repeated scans of my chest and heart, and typed opinions from different specialists. *Partial collapsing of the lung. Heart attack. Cholestasis. Multiple organ failure. Global cerebral ischemia. Subarachnoid hemorrhage.* Seeing my injuries listed so coldly, I broke down crying. I grabbed the files, carried them into my office, and shoved them inside a drawer of my writing desk, where they've sat these past two decades. Every few months, prompted by the latest rendering of my memoir, I've pulled the files out and paged through them. Over the years, I've highlighted important dates and facts in neon orange and purple. Along the margins, I've added my notes and questions, as I do when reading great works of literature. My afflictions are written in cryptic medicalese. The language becomes even more obscure when, quite often, those technical words are abbreviated or stated as an acronym. It's clear from these rushed notes that doctors were speaking to other doctors, asking for second opinions, urgently demanding referrals to specialists. These files were not meant for me.

If I persisted in cracking the code, it was largely because this wasn't the first time I felt barred from a text that was meant to provide me answers. Verses in the Qur'an can be frustratingly vague, elliptical, even repetitive. Less written narrative and more oral poetry delivered in an archaic Arabic few understand, these verses have sometimes required me to spend months on a single term and its multiple historical uses, reading and rereading passages, until the intention and meaning emerged from what was once mystifying.

Similarly, it was in returning again and again to those medical terms and researching the abbreviations and numbers—values, ranges, blood tests that were performed every four hours around the clock, many with one word in all caps above the results, ABNORMAL—that it all came together.

As it turns out, Scott and I—two creative writers with no medical background and with only the help of a mass-produced pregnancy book—had in fact diagnosed my condition correctly. I'd suffered from a multisystem disorder called preeclampsia. While its exact cause is unknown, researchers believe that, after fertilization, when the blastocyst (the early stage of an embryo) doesn't implant correctly, the placenta begins to send out distress signals. The distress signals are in the form of molecules that get shot into the mother's bloodstream. These molecules damage the blood vessels, which start to leak fluid into tissues, causing her to become puffy and swollen. Blood pressure starts rising. Healthy kidneys have specialized types of vascular cells to filter out waste from the blood, but the distress signals instead allow the kidneys to pass abnormally large waste through. Big molecules called proteins are released into the urine, which is what the OB checks for at each prenatal visit with the reagent strip that gets dipped into the mother's urine sample. Protein in urine means your kidneys aren't functioning properly.

But in 15 to 20 percent of patients, which is where I fell, preeclampsia starts in the liver, which means symptoms other than hypertension and proteinuria are present. For me, the blood vessels in my brain were starting to leak, causing my brain to swell. I began having headaches and vision changes, minor, unnoticeable strokes.

Although preeclampsia commonly involves the kidneys and vasculature (blood vessels), when it's left to fester on its own, as it was with me, the disease escalates to damage the central nervous system (which consists of the brain and spinal cord), and so leads to seizures. In its most lethal manifestation, the disease leaves nothing intact, decimates the entire body, from the cells lining the blood vessels to the major organs: kidneys, liver, heart, lungs, and brain.

Without the intervention I kept begging my OBs for, my preeclampsia turned into its most lethal form: hemolysis, elevated liver enzymes, and low platelets.

HELLP syndrome.

# 16

The same night I delivered my son and was transferred down to the neuro-ICU and hooked up to life-support machines, all efforts focused on keeping me alive, Ishmael nearly died himself. Preeclampsia is often described as a rejection of the baby. In a normal pregnancy, the placenta creates the right atmosphere for the mother's body to successfully nourish the fetus. When it's not implanted correctly, however, the distress signals aggravate her immune system, which then begins attacking the baby as it might cancer cells or a newly transplanted organ, trying to get rid of this foreign entity.

So, for nine months, while gestating and developing, my son was swimming in the pregnancy disease. Instead of being nourished, he was slowly being starved. He began his life by confronting death, fending off attacks on his survival. He was born sickly and underweight. He performed miserably on his first Apgar test. Up in the newborn nursery, he was lying alone while the medical staff fussed over me when, too lethargic to breathe, he simply stopped. By the time the nurse noticed what was happening and rushed him to the neonatal ICU, his body had turned blue. It suddenly seemed that Scott was going to lose both his wife and his son within minutes of each other.

With both of us now effectively stationed in an ICU, seven floors apart, the doctors and nurses put their heads together and decided that it would be best if Scott did not leave the hospital. They assigned him a private room on the maternity ward, the room that had originally been set aside for me to recover in after the delivery. As the medical staff saw it, once Scott had moved into the hospital, he would be accessible at all hours to give consent on any necessary emergency medical procedure or, as was likely to happen in my case, simply to say his last goodbyes.

Of course these are not my memories. These memories belong to Scott, to my parents and two brothers, to my friend Naomi. I heard these accounts much later, after I emerged from the coma and after I was sent home to convalesce, my mind so blank it felt like I had swallowed a pitch-black sky. So others filled my emptiness with their memories. To help ground me, they said. To fill me in on what happened during the five days I was in a coma, they said. In the initial stages of brain recovery, I was impressionable. My mind was an arid desert. Without the usual clutter in my head, without memories and impressions and thoughts of my own, others' memories became etched into my gray matter as my own experiences. I am at once on life support in the neuro-ICU and also standing over my son as he stops breathing in the nursery. I am both lying absolutely still in a coma and also frantically rushing up and down several flights of the hospital building, from the fifteenth- and top-floor maternity ward down to the seventh-floor neurology ward and back up again. Every story I heard about my son's first experiences sparked another neuron in my brain like a star suddenly lighting up in the dark, expansive sky.

*Paradise*

## 17

When my mom was pregnant with me in 1969, she was reading an Urdu novel whose heroine had captivated her for being bold and courageous—qualities that she, at the young age of twenty-four, married and already the mother to my older brother, was eager to develop in herself. My dad had just submitted an application to the U.S. Embassy in Madras for an immigration visa. A civil engineer who'd graduated at the top of his class from prestigious Osmania University, he satisfied the strict immigration criteria requiring a college degree, so there was a good chance he'd be approved. As much as my mom wanted to go, she also dreaded the thought. Immigrating would require the two to do what no one in the history of our family had done before, not even after Partition. They would have to uproot and move out of our ancestral home, saying goodbye to their siblings and aging parents, their local streets and neighborhoods, everything they'd ever known. And since my dad was planning to go first to secure an apartment, it meant my mom, who'd never left Hyderabad, not even to visit other cities in India, would have to make the long, complicated journey across the world alone, with two young babies in tow—which is exactly what she eventually did.

The name of the novel's heroine who inspired my mom was Samina. Unlike the name Ishmael that I chose for my son, the name Samina has no connections to Islamic theology. There are no narratives in the Qur'an concerning anyone named Samina. In fact, in Arabic, the meaning of the name is so derogatory that Arabic speakers who meet me for the first time often ask why my parents chose to name me "fatty." *Were you overweight when you were born?*

In spite of my mom calling me Samina, it never became my official name. As Hyderabadi Muslims, my parents accepted that naming their own child was a serious duty that they weren't allowed to perform. Nor would they take on such a responsibility when they knew that, according to the Prophet, a name directly impacts the child's development. For this reason, after the birth of a child, an imam is the one who consults the Qur'an and carefully selects a name based on the date of birth and the alignment of the stars. My two brothers were both given fortuitous names in accordance with this tradition. After I was born, however, my parents resisted informing the imam for as long as they could get away with it. They didn't have it in themselves to formally acknowledge my birth date. As my mom has explained to me over the years in the accusatory tone she uses whenever we speak about my birth, as though I had control over its timing, both of my brothers were born on blessed days. Whereas

I had come into this world on the grimmest day in Islamic history: the day, a mere fifty years after our beloved Prophet had died, when his last living family members, including his precious grandson Hussein, had been rounded up and brutally slain by enemies to Islam.

When I imagine my parents bringing me home from the hospital days after I was born, their auto-rickshaw zigzagging through ancient alleyways toward my dad's rambling house in the Old City, I see the neighborhood exactly as I've seen it each year around my birthday when I was growing up. Overnight, practically every man, woman, and child living in the district shrouds themselves in black. Green flags with white Arabic script declaring "There is no god but Allah" are erected over low-slung, concrete houses. TVs are turned off. Music is banned. Laughter is stifled. Residents gather together at mosques and in homes. Sitting cross-legged on cold, hard cement floors, every inch of which have been covered in white sheets, both men and women give themselves over to an imam's fiery sermon. Similar to Christian passion plays, which dramatize the suffering, death, and resurrection of Christ, these chronicle the sad events of Hussein's last days.

Knowing that my life was connected across time and space to these ancient tragedies, my parents turned to Old City superstitions to try to protect me. In the early days after I was born, they sought out the most reputable witch doctors and faith healers and carried out the wildest of rituals. They bought the plumpest, healthiest black chickens in the marketplace only to bring the fowls home and slit their throats at my tiny, newborn feet, spraying my toes with blood, before casting the fat carcasses onto the local dump heap. They placed eggs near my head while I slept and, in the morning, my ayah carried these eggs far from the house, far from me, and pitched them into some random alleyway, breaking the shells open, releasing bad energies back into the universe. An entire science exists around the therapeutic powers of the Qur'an, and my parents seeped verses in a tub of hot water and bathed me. They had prayers typed in the tiniest fonts possible onto miniature scrolls that were then rolled up and squeezed inside silver amulets, tied with red thread around my wrists and neck, encircling my belly. Kohl was applied heavily around my eyes to ward off the evil eye. Fourteen days after my birth, my head was carefully shaved, and my newborn hair weighed on a jeweler's scale. The weight of the silky strands was doubled in gold and that gold was gifted to my ayah. In my baby photos, I am a strange-looking creature. Bald, black-eyed, and tied up with red threads and silver amulets.

Only when I was six months old and my dad's immigration visa to the U.S. was approved and he was invited by the U.S. Embassy in Madras to submit documents for his wife and children so that we could accompany him to the U.S. were my parents forced to summon an imam. My birth stars proved to be as ominous to him as to my parents, so the imam spent extra time sitting with the Qur'an and reciting prayers in order to bestow a name that might, at best, counteract some of the misfortune the stars foretold, or, if that wasn't possible, a name that would, at the very least, shield me from the worst that was destined to come.

With a heavy heart, my dad wrote the religious name the imam had chosen onto the embassy documents. From those papers, that name was transferred onto the Indian passport I used to immigrate to Minneapolis in January 1971, when I was just under two years old, with my mom and older brother. From there, that name went onto my Minneapolis school records, and eventually onto my driver's license, my Certificate of Naturalization, and finally onto my U.S. passport. Now, it's that official name I use when I file my taxes. My religious name—the name the imam selected to entrust me to God's protection—has become my legal name, the name used by my former classmates and by government workers, those who speak English. But that name, which is linked to my birth stars, is not a name my parents have ever used. They instead call me Samina. And because my parents call me Samina, my relatives and friends back home in Hyderabad, and everyone who speaks Urdu, calls me Samina. Originating from the name of a flower, in Urdu the name Samina means "precious." In my parents' way of thinking, not using the name the imam bestowed and not documenting my birthday was effectively obscuring my existence. By hiding me away, by making me invisible, by essentially concealing my existence behind a hijab, they were trying to keep God's attention from being drawn to me.

If I was never born, how could I ever die?

# 18

By the end of my second night in the neuro-ICU, my kidneys had failed. My liver had failed. My heart was sputtering about, damaged, throwing off enzymes. I'd been given two blood transfusions and yet my blood platelet count had plummeted from a normal range of 250,000 to a mere seven and my blood still wasn't clotting. But all that was secondary. What concerned my neurologist most was the acute damage to my brain. Hundreds of strokes, he guessed, a galaxy of shooting and popping blood vessels. The internal pressure was inflating my brain like a helium balloon, expanding, expanding, expanding until the soft ridges of tissue were pressing up against the hard inside of the skull. Medications to reduce the swelling weren't working. Given the extent of the trauma, the doctor told my parents and husband that if I was lucky, I would die. If not, one of them would have to make my end-of-life decisions. At the age of twenty-nine, I was newly married and pregnant with our first child. I had thought my life was just beginning. It had never occurred to me to draw up a living will.

"Don't think of the machines as extending her life," the neurologist cautioned my family in that gentle voice of his, "but rather as prolonging her death."

# 19

"Don't listen to those doctors," my mother was cautioning me, her voice unmistakable in my ear. "They don't know what they're talking about."

The memory is fragmented, lasting just a few seconds. My mom was telling me that she and my dad were praying for me, that they had arranged for an imam to carry the Qur'an to the top of a holy mountain right outside Hyderabad and recite it in my name so that God, whom we all knew to be all-compassionate and all-merciful—*al rahman, al rahim*—would grant me a second chance at life.

I had no idea why she was telling me this. I didn't know my son had stopped breathing. I didn't know I'd experienced a grand mal seizure twenty minutes after delivering him. I was in a coma. I was intubated. I was on life support. Stationed inside a cramped, curtained space in the neuro-ICU, I was watched over by a private nurse around the clock. The only reason I was able to hear what my mother was telling me was because, despite everything that had broken down in my body, I was experiencing a passing moment of lucidity. It couldn't have come at a worse time.

"I stayed up all night and prayed for you," she was saying. "If Allah was going to take you from me, I'd know, don't you think? I'm your mother. I'd feel it, don't you think?"

I couldn't tell if she was asking me for reassurance or stating a fact.

She cleared her throat and suddenly began speaking slowly, as she did when she wanted to make sure I understood what she was telling me. "Nothing is going to happen to you. Do you hear? Your father and I ordered sheep to be slaughtered in your name. We're going to serve mutton biryani at every orphanage in Hyderabad. You'll see, nothing is going to happen to you. Allah is greater and greatest, Allahu Akbar. Those doctors don't know what they're talking about. Remember what your dad and I have taught you. Remember the mercy God showed Abraham and Ismail. Keep your faith in Allah."

I knew instantly the significance of my mom's words, the magnitude of the steps being taken. She was reminding me of Abraham's willingness to sacrifice his son. She and my dad were slaughtering sheep as a way of asking God to spare my life. What could have happened to me to get my mom to say such things? My mom must have been touching me. I must have been in pain. The lower lobes of my lungs were filled with liquid. A tube was shoved down my throat. Stiff plastic cords were injected into my arms, my inner thighs, up my groin. There was so much liquid coursing through my body, bloating my organs and flesh, that my nose appeared to have sunk into my face. But other than her words, I was aware of nothing. Not the beeping of the machines that were hooked up to my body, running in the place of my organs. Not the sound of my strained breathing.

I tried to open my eyes. I tried to speak. I was angry. Why is everyone praying for me? I wanted to ask her. I don't need your prayers, I wanted to shout. My body wouldn't respond. I was shut in. My anger turned to panic. And just then, just as terror was overtaking me, the moment of lucidity passed. Like a match being blown out.

I sank right back under the layers of unconsciousness.

# 20

They say that when you're about to die, your life flashes before your eyes. In those fleeting, final seconds of life, you see everyone who's meant anything to you, your parents, your friends, those you've loved and those you've betrayed. Your strengths and your failings are projected before you so that as you take your last breaths you can weigh and assess and conclude. Did I live my best life? Or did I let my days waste away?

When my organs were shutting down one after another, little lights in my body switching off, did my life flash before my eyes? My son had just been delivered with the help of forceps. The cardiologist was pestering me to tell him how many fingers he was holding up. In my medical file, it states that during this examination I suffered a grand mal seizure. That's when Scott saw my body convulsing.

But that's not my memory. So, what is the last thing I remember?

I remember thinking that it didn't matter how many fingers the doctor was holding up when my body was being painfully ripped apart. I remember trying to keep my eyes open, to get my mouth to move to answer the cardiologist, and just then, just as I was doing my best to speak, just as I was trying my hardest to stay alert, I remember something miraculous happened. Like God intervening. There I'd been, begging the doctors for pain meds. Then, suddenly, I didn't need them anymore. A spring erupted inside me, releasing a kind of organic pain relief. I could feel it bubbling up from my feet, rising through my calves and thighs, my pelvis, more effective and complete than anesthesia. It rippled through me, relaxing my muscles, numbing my agony.

The shout to clear the room, the commotion that ensued, my son being rushed out—I have no memory of any of it. From my pelvis up through the constriction in my chest and then up the back of my stiff neck and up farther still, finally, to my exploding head, I remember my nerves switching off to the pain, the seductive nature of this self-destruction. Everything relaxed at once. I lost control of my body, gave in. Gave up.

In that final moment, I didn't see my parents' faces. I didn't think of my son. I wasn't filled with regret over lost dreams, or gratitude for what I'd been given. My life didn't flash before my eyes because it's simply not possible for the mind to step back from the significance of those final seconds. When death arrives, every neuron and every cell and every sense in your body is aware of it. You're not thinking of anyone else. I didn't consider how my death might destroy my parents. I didn't worry that my son would grow up not knowing his mom. It didn't matter to me how Scott would cope in my absence. Would he forget about me? Would he fall in love and marry again? Would some woman I didn't know end up raising my son? These are the concerns of the living.

Death is a selfish moment. When it arrives, it seizes your attention, monopolizing it, and tunes out everything and everyone around you. As in meditation, your attention turns inward. You feel the darkness creeping through your body, switching off nerves, shutting down organs. It's something you've never felt before, an entirely new sensation. And yet there's no doubt in your mind what's happening. Death is coy. It seduces you, whispers its name into your ear, the core of your being. The process doesn't frighten you. It captivates you. You don't shrink away from death. You embrace it.

The last memory I have, right as my body fell limp, is of smiling in relief.

## 21

Whenever people hear that I was in a coma, they immediately want to know what it was like. They're fascinated. Could I hear my family talking to me? Could I feel them touching me? Is being in a coma anything like being in a deep sleep? In recent years, I've read research asserting that a coma patient may benefit from hearing voices of loved ones, that these familiar tones help to bring a patient more quickly to consciousness.

I'm told that my parents and my brothers and my husband and Naomi stood for hours around my bed—but I couldn't tell you with any confidence that they were in fact there. My mom is not a physically affectionate person. While growing up, she never hugged me or said she loved me. If I tried to touch her, she'd snatch her body away. She'd hiss at me. I approached her like I did a wild animal, cautiously. When she saw me lying unconscious in the neuro-ICU, hooked up to machines, and she decided to whisper into my ear that everything was going to be all right, that I should place my faith in Allah, did she at last take my hand into her own? I couldn't tell you for sure. Did my dad kiss my forehead as he's always done when he greets me? Did the two of them finally feel defeated by my inauspicious birthday?

When the neurologist explained the EVD procedure, as Scott remembers it, he also said that anesthesia wouldn't be necessary while drilling the hole through my skull, not in my condition. To keep me from sinking deeper into the layers of unconsciousness, the nurses and doctors frequently yelled into my face at the top of their lungs. They routinely pinched my fingernails with all their strength. Their medical methods were torture. Scott refused to watch. My body was already suffering so much, and he felt they were hurting me more. He got up and left the room.

But I felt nothing. No sensation whatsoever. It was only much later when I was discharged and sent home that I noticed my fingernails were black and blue, like those on a corpse.

## 22

In one of my earliest memories, my mom had just learned about her father's death. I must have been five years old, around the age when the brain has developed enough to retain long-term memory. My parents had immigrated to the U.S. four years earlier in 1971. Our family had moved once during that period, from a tiny one-bedroom apartment in South Minneapolis, where my parents, older brother, and I had all slept squeezed together on a queen-size bed (my younger brother hadn't been born yet) to what now seemed a palatial two-bedroom town house. My mom had walked me home from school. On our way into the house, she'd fetched the mail. A light green aerogram from India had arrived, as one did every month. With a smile on her face, she tore it open the moment we stepped into the house. The letter was written in Urdu, the script moving from right to left, transporting her like jet streams back across the ocean to her home in Hyderabad. She read the letter stand-ing in the doorway to my bedroom, her back to me. I had just changed out of my school clothes and wanted to go out and play, so I was trying to squeeze past her. I remember she was wearing a sari as she always did, unwilling to expose her legs in the miniskirts and shirtdresses that were popular in that era. Our hippie neighbors didn't realize my mom was conditioned to be modest and they found her saris and diamond nose ring to be unbelievably "groovy."

While I was trying to squeeze past her, I heard a sharp intake of breath and then silence. Was it the gasp or the silence that rooted me to the spot? All at once, I knew something terrible had happened. Her body slumped against the doorway. I was squeezed in tight between her soft flesh and the hard wooden doorframe, but I knew better than to move. She didn't tell me then that my grandfather had died. Later that evening, I overheard her informing my dad when he came home from work. There was muffled crying as she wrapped herself in a black sari of mourning. We didn't return to Hyderabad for the funeral. My mom didn't think it would be worth making the long trip. As a woman, she wouldn't be allowed near her father's grave to witness his body being lowered into the ground. While the men went off to bury her father, she'd be stuck back at his house, grieving from afar, just as easily as she could grieve from her own home in Minneapolis.

Not attending proved to be more painful than my mom anticipated. The day of the funeral, she didn't pick me up from school. I remember waiting with my older brother outside the front entrance well after the last student had gone home. Not knowing what else to do, my brother and I finally made the brave decision to walk the few blocks by ourselves. We found her in bed, her bedroom door locked. We could hear her crying.

When we knocked, she ignored us. That night, on his way back from work, my dad picked up McDonald's hamburgers for dinner. My mom stayed locked in the bedroom for three days. When she suddenly reappeared in the school pickup line, she was still dressed in the black sari, now wrinkled and smelling of perspiration and grief. Her hair was knotted and greasy, her skin tinged a sickening yellow. She looked hollowed out.

My mom believes the tradition of barring women from attending burials is based in Islam. When I was nineteen and in Hyderabad and my ayah, Fiza, passed away, we argued about it. My ayah had been my nursemaid and was like a second mother to me. Up until her death, she'd fed me with her hands, she'd bathed me in the hammam, she'd stood up for me when I needed. When my parents married me off and sent me to live with my in-laws, my ayah moved in with me. I couldn't imagine not attending her burial. I was bereft. I wailed and screamed, reminding my mom that missing her dad's funeral had only intensified her suffering, then went so far as to accuse her of being jealous of my attachment to my ayah, but nothing I said would make her relent. She kept repeating that it was improper for women to attend a burial.

Now I understand that it's not my mom's fault for believing this. Even when King Hussein of Jordan was buried, his widow, Queen Noor, was left grieving in a palace far from the grave site. No woman attended the king's funeral or burial. But for some reason I couldn't identify, a decade after Fiza passed, during the years of my recovery, my mind kept returning to her death. Something was bothering me. I thought it might be the fight I'd had with my mom. Fiza had been with my mom's family since she and my mom were four years old. They had grown up together in my grandfather's home. They'd played together as children. They'd developed into women alongside each other. It wasn't just me who had a bond with Fiza; there'd been a strong sisterly love between the two women. Despite their ties, my mom hadn't gone to Fiza's burial and, worse, she hadn't gone to her own dad's burial, which meant—and this was the point nagging at me—had I died, she wouldn't have come to mine.

Outraged, I did what I've done most of my life and turned to the literature. If God was truly merciful, as my mom was always reminding me, as I recited before every prayer—*al rahman, al rahim*—why would such a god deny women this mercy? What I discovered was that the Prophet himself was opposed to these traditions, which must have predated Islam. According to historical narrations, when the Prophet was being laid to rest, several women from his family were present, including his wife, Ayesha, and his daughter, Fatima. Before he passed, he'd even left instructions that women from the community be allowed to attend his burial, in a section behind his family and friends. In direct contradiction to his wishes, several decades after the Prophet's death, Muslim scholars prohibited women from attending burials—and even legitimized the practice by attributing it to Islam. Women, these scholars argued, were so bereft they often showed up to funerals without a head covering. They went crazy with grief and tended to rip their clothing or cut off their hair or scratch at their own faces and wail. They attracted too much attention to themselves. For the sake of modesty—for their own sakes—women were barred.

Yet the demonstrations of grief these scholars are referring to are not specific to women. In the Arabian region of that era, it was thought that the performative aspects of mourning honored the memory of the deceased. In the Biblical story of Mordecai in mourning, the book of Esther says that Mordecai "mourned when he learned of all that had been done. He tore his clothes, put on a sackcloth and wiped ash onto his body. Then he went out into the city, wailing loudly and bitterly," (Esther 4:1). The Mishnah quotes the Rabbi Judah ruling that for a wife's funeral "even the poorest in Israel should hire not less than two flutes and one wailing woman," (Ketubot 4:4). In Rabbinic times, funeral processions were led by lamenting female mourners, often professionals who knew how to put on a public show of grief.

When I told my mom what I'd learned, she didn't take it well. I wasn't a scholar, she reminded me. I was just a creative writer. She questioned the veracity of my sources and accused me of always trying to "feminize Islam." We argued, but I didn't yell as I had after my ayah died. I simply repeated what I'd uncovered. Finally, when we had cooled down a bit, she asked me, "Why are you bringing this up?"

How could I tell her what was going through my head, this hypothetical? If I die, I want you to be there when they bury me. So instead I said, "We could have gone to Fiza's burial."

My mom instantly intuited what I really meant. I heard a sharp intake of her breath and noticed a slumping of her shoulders. Even her voice softened. But I could tell that nothing I'd said, not even this, had persuaded her to change her mind.

"Well," she repeated, "it doesn't matter now, does it?"

# 23

As my parents tell it, by the end of my third day in the neuro-ICU, Scott was staggering about in a state of shock, barely keeping it together. My brain was still swelling, not responding to medications. The neurologist had decided it would be best to drill a hole in my skull and drain the excess fluid.

"The procedure is called an EVD," he explained to my family. "We'll make an inch-long incision just behind the hairline and drill a hole into the skull. Given her state," he added, "she won't need any sedation." Did the doctor really say that? Or is that just how Scott's memory recast the horror of it all?

While the doctors were urging Scott to give his permission for the EVD, my mom was coaxing him to perform the Islamic birth rituals for Ishmael. Numbed to the core, he was unable to do either.

## 24

When I was growing up, my parents told me that my life story was being compiled into a book by two angels. Known in Islamic tradition as *kiraman katibin*, these honorable scribes were appointed at the time of birth and remained till death. One sat on my left shoulder, carefully taking note of every misdeed and foul word and sin, while the other sat on my right shoulder, mercifully recording every kind act and benevolent utterance and repentance.

The Qur'an mentions these noble recorders on at least two occasions with a terrifying "they know whatever you do," [82: 10-12]. My parents routinely reminded my two brothers and me of this fact as a way of disciplining us. My mom didn't think of it as scaring me into compliance, but instead as inspiring me to do better.

"When you die and face God, what will you say when God asks why you skipped your prayers today?"

"If you hurt your brother's feelings by excluding him and

making him cry like this, how will you face God's judgment after you die?"

"Don't let your friends convince you to drink alcohol at the party. Remember, you will have to endure God's displeasure on the Day of Reckoning."

Even from a young age, I never doubted that God would come to know of every transgression, no matter how insignificant, because, on the Day of Judgment, the *kiraman katibin* would present God with an accounting of my life, called the Book of Deeds. From these pages, my virtuous and unvirtuous acts would be extracted and divided up, weighed on a heavenly scale called *mizan* to determine which was heavier. It was on that fateful day that I, too, would be handed this meticulous documentation to read and understand God's judgment of me. A narrow, slippery bridge known as Sirat spans the torturous depths of hell. If I'd been rewarded with entrance into paradise, I'd be able to cross the bridge with great speed and agility and peace of mind. If not, I'd slip and tumble, condemned to the fire.

When my labor contractions were thirty minutes apart and I was anxiously riding the elevator up to the fifteenth-floor labor and delivery ward, convinced that I wouldn't make it back down, it was during those terrifying moments that my life did in fact flash before my eyes. There were things I'd done, such as divorcing my first husband and, later, marrying Scott, a man outside my race and faith, which had displeased my parents. And they'd warned me that displeasing them meant that I'd displeased Allah too. These were the kinds of memories that came to me, moments when I'd been told I was an errant daughter. A disappointment. Although I'd been steadfast in these decisions, there was something about the possibility that I might soon be facing God with my Book of Deeds that made me fear my feet would slip when crossing the Sirat bridge.

# 25

My dad and I weren't on speaking terms when I delivered my son. We hadn't talked in three years, not since I called him from San Francisco to announce that I was marrying Scott. It didn't matter to my dad that Scott and I were planning a ceremony at the mosque. He knew that Scott wasn't Muslim and, equally offensive to him, that Scott was a poet I'd met during my MFA program in the Pacific Northwest, so he forbade me from marrying him. The notion of an equivalent match is the basis of an arranged marriage; a mate is selected who is similar in background, economically and socially and religiously. Whether the couple is attracted to each other or even in love isn't relevant. In my dad's mind, Scott wouldn't be able to financially support me in the way I'd grown accustomed to. My marriage would leave me wanting. And because it would leave me wanting, my marriage was doomed. He told me as much.

But I refused to back down. I told my dad I was marrying Scott whether or not he gave his blessing. Angry that I was defying him, he went so far as to mock Scott, asking if he'd landed a six-figure deal to sell his poetry collection. I dug in my heels even deeper. I'd already done things his way, I reminded him. I'd already agreed to marry the man my parents had chosen. The man they'd thought was such a good fit. And look where that had gotten me. I told my dad it was now my turn to choose. If my marriage failed, it would be on me. Before he could say anything more, I hung up. And that action, my shocking disrespect to cut the phone line, to shut him up, shut him down, led him to cut me out of his life.

So he was still in Minneapolis, and we were still estranged, when my mom called him to say the delivery hadn't gone as planned.

"What do you mean?" he asked.

"Things took a bad turn," she repeated just as vaguely as before.

Finally, my younger brother, a medical resident in neurosurgery at the time, took the phone from my mom's hand and assaulted my dad with the news she couldn't bring herself to say. He explained that my dad had better get to the hospital fast if he wanted to say his last goodbyes.

In the frantic rush to the Minneapolis airport, I'm told that my dad broke down crying. My brother's words were spinning in his head. While driving, my dad was praying out loud to Allah for mercy. Then he was lamenting. Then he was on the phone to India, ordering sheep to be slaughtered, hiring an imam to climb a holy mountain with the Qur'an. He wasn't paying attention to the road. His car swerved.

Horns blared. Other drivers flipped him off as they maneu-
vered around him. Before he could stop himself, he'd pulled
over and parked alongside the busy highway, the sound of
cars zooming past reverberating up through the leather car
seat. He knew he was in danger of missing his flight. But he
couldn't get himself to keep driving to the Minneapolis airport. He was ashamed. Why had he held a grudge for three
years against his own child?

He confessed all this to my mom. At what point during
my recovery did she confide in me? All I know for sure is that
I've never seen my dad cry, not even when his own dad died
and we flew back to Hyderabad so he could attend the funeral.
I was about seven years old, and I remember being confused
about why we had made the long journey because, during
the funeral ceremony, my dad refused to enter the mosque.
I was still young enough to be allowed at the funeral, in spite
of being female, and was sitting cross-legged on the marble
floor between my two brothers. It was the first funeral I'd
ever attended and I'd been anxious, not sure how I'd handle being in a room full of weeping men. Having grown up
far away in Minneapolis, I wasn't close enough to my grandfather to feel any kind of real sorrow. But it turned out that
the only men at the funeral expressing grief were those who
didn't know my grandfather at all. They had no connection to
our family. They were professional mourners who sat at the
very back of the mosque, making up a final row. From there,
they wailed powerfully for everyone to hear. They wailed so
others wouldn't. They wailed because those truly grieving

were expected to remain quietly dignified. I noticed my uncles giving these mourners money—not as payment, I later learned, but in alms.

At the time, the entire scene confused me. I ran out of the mosque in search of my dad. I thought he'd escaped outside to cry alone. I found him pacing the narrow courtyard, his hands clasped behind his back, staring at the ground as he walked. Unlike what I'd expected, he looked stoic, maybe even a little impatient, as though he wanted to be done with the funeral so we could head home. When he caught sight of me, he quickly looked away, not wanting the intrusion. As much as I wanted to go to him, I sat on the steps several feet away and watched him pace.

When I think of my dad mourning me, I wish the image that came to mind was of him breaking down crying on the side of a busy freeway. But, instead, it's this memory of him in the courtyard, turning his face away.

# 26

Of the five days I was in a coma, I have two memories, both fractured and incomplete. In the first, my eyes are open. I see the neurologist and the nurse and the line of medical residents lined up around the foot of my bed. One of their torturous methods must have achieved what they'd hoped and awoken me. But I wasn't really awake. I merely had my eyes open. My memory starts after the action has already begun. My body has been propped up in bed but without a will of its own I find myself awkwardly lurching forward, on a beeline to landing flat on my face. I am in the middle of shouting for help. I can hear my own voice. But I've no control over what I'm saying. The person who is speaking has somehow separated from the person who is witnessing her speaking. I'm listening to myself as I might to someone else in the room. Removed from myself, I'm taken aback by my own tone, which stings of an accusation—I'm impugning the medical staff for failing me. I'm saying exactly what I'd wanted to say but couldn't at the time of the actual delivery. It's clear I feel abandoned.

"Will someone please help me get my baby out!" I shout. "Why are you all so useless!"

My voice booms in the solemn neuro-ICU. Desperation and fear have infused my words with force and vitality. I don't sound like a woman in a coma. But clearly the internal clock has stopped. My body is still back in the delivery room, still desperate to get the obstetrician's attention. Still desperate to deliver my son. Then my face flattens against the mattress as I hit the bed and I am out again and the memory ends just as abruptly as it began, the neurons extinguished like a flare burning out.

The second memory is the one of my mom whispering in my ear, telling me not to worry, that the whole of the Qur'an was being read for me, from cover to cover in the darkness of one night. The significance of her words lit up my brain in panic. The Qur'an consists of 114 chapters. The Qur'an was revealed in stages over the course of twenty-three years. The Qur'an is written in a difficult archaic Arabic dialect. To help make it easier to consume, the Qur'an is divided into thirty parts so that one part can be recited each day for the thirty days of Ramadan. There was only one reason to try to get through the entire text in one night.

To my family and to the medical professionals, the first of these two episodes, the one in which my eyes are open, the one in which I have no control of my body or of my speech, must have been alarming. And yet it's the second episode, the one no one witnessed, the one where my eyes are closed but my consciousness is alert, that unnerves me even today. I can't help but wonder why I flickered into lucidity at this very moment, why I was meant to hear of my own demise.

## 27

To understand the Qur'an, you have to understand the Old Testament. Nearly fifty prophets mentioned in the Qur'an first made an appearance there, so the Qur'an doesn't waste pages retelling their stories. Adam and Eve, Jesus and Mary, Moses and Abraham: I first read their entire accounts in my Bible studies class in Catholic school. In fact, back when the Islamic scriptures were first being introduced, the earliest listeners scornfully dismissed the revelations as "tales of the ancients" (6:25). And they dismissed the Prophet, whom they knew had come across these Jewish and Christian narratives as a young trader traveling the lengthy Silk Road. The Qur'an has no qualms admitting to these intentional overlaps, referring to itself as a "reminder" of the right path. Similar to the other two Abrahamic faiths, that right path, it promises, will lead to the soul's resurrection and eternal existence in paradise.

When I tell people my story, no matter their religious background, they usually want to know the same thing. Did

I experience something transcendent? Or do we just become compost? I imagine that those who ask me want assurances that there's something more, that the religious stories passed down to us about an afterlife are based in some truth. As it turns out, I didn't have cause to worry about slipping off Sirat bridge into the cavernous abyss of hell. As I later discovered, that bridge is never mentioned in the Qur'an. It's not officially part of the Muslim theology of the afterlife. Like the prohibition against women attending burials, this concept was introduced by Islamic scholars in the years following the Prophet's death. The Silk Roads, which Muhammed traveled as a young trader in the years before he became a prophet, were a vast network of land and sea routes used from about 200 BCE to 1400 CE. Approximately 4,600 miles long, stretching across immense deserts and over tall mountains, these trading routes extended from as far east as Japan then traveled west through Xi'an, China, Afghanistan, Iran, Iraq, down south through India, and up north through Turkey, Greece, and Italy. Traders, armies, religious pilgrims, great scholars, and travel writers like Ibn Battuta all bartered and exchanged textiles, spices, gems, animals, and even religious ideas along these routes. The great movement of people and thought helped to spread Buddhism, Christianity, Islam, and, of course, those religions that far predated them. It wasn't difficult to trace where the idea of the Sirat bridge might have come from.

In the second millennium BCE, the Persian prophet Zarathustra (Zoroaster in Greek) founded what is considered the first monotheistic faith in history, Zoroastrianism. The

Zoroastrians' concept of the afterlife is written into their scripture, the Avesta. Once the dominant religion in Iran, Zoroastrians now live predominantly in India, where I grew up knowing Zoroastrians as the Parsees—Persians. Like in Tibetan Buddhism—another belief system that spread along the Silk Road—Zoroastrians give their dead a sky burial. Corpses are left on circular, flat-topped towers to be eaten by vultures. For the first three days after the person has passed, Zoroastrians believe the soul hovers near the body while its deeds are judged and weighed. On the morning of the fourth day, the soul is guided to a bridge. The Chinvat Bridge, as it's called, spans the abyss of the living and the dead. While crossing the bridge, good souls encounter a beautiful maiden and enter paradise, the House of Songs, transforming into angel-like beings. Bad souls are attacked by an evil witch and tumble off the bridge into the dark loneliness of hell, the House of Lies.

Our brains don't seem to be designed to fathom our non-existence. For months after the coma, my own brain kept its injuries hidden from me. My frontal cortex was damaged, impairing my speech and memory and my higher functions of thought and imagination, making me incapable of caring for myself, and yet my brain convinced me that I was absolutely fine. I was in radiant health! If I was unable to track what others were saying, unable to answer the neurologists' persistent questions, it was because there was something wrong with them. I was the smartest person in the room. Minutes after I emerged from the coma, minutes away from death, I was already convinced of my immortality.

# 28

The same afternoon that my dad flew in from Minneapolis, he followed Scott up to the neonatal ICU and took a seat next to Ishmael's incubator. He'd just visited me in the neuro-ICU. Although he'd tried to hide it, he'd been horrified by the sight of me. Nothing about me was recognizable to him. The wires and tubes, my body bloated and unconscious. My stillness set him into motion. He realized he had to do what I couldn't do and perform the birth rituals.

At least, this is what I'm imagining happened, in the absence of my dad's own testimony. There are no pictures from those five days, and my mom and my brothers and Scott and Naomi each have contradictory memories of how events unfolded. So my brain has patched together gaps in my timeline with bits of stories others have shared and photographs taken after I emerged from the coma, as well as my own imaginings.

"Ismail," my dad must have said in the neonatal ICU, tenderly lifting him from the incubator and holding his grandson for the first time. He must have appraised him. The wispy blond hair and gray-blue eyes. The body emaciated and malnourished from the eclampsia. His tiny ribs protruding outward. His diaper drooping down from his thin waist, hanging loosely between his scrawny thighs. One delicate hand covered by what looked to be a gauze mitten. Around his other hand, running the full length of his tiny forearm, an IV line. Clear plastic tape wrapped around his fingers and around his hand and arm, down to the elbow, keeping the tube in place. A bloodied cotton ball taped around his tiny fingertips. As my dad held my son's frail body against his own chest so that my son would remember to imitate the rhythm of his breathing, I imagine the words already running through his head. In Islam, right after a child is born and handed over to the mother, the first words a newborn hears are from the Qur'an. Just as baptism is a declaration of faith in the Gospel and an admission into the Christian Church, my son would only become a Muslim after hearing the declaration of his faith. *Ashhadan la Ilaha illa'lah . . . I bear witness that there is no god but God.*

# 29

Around the time my dad visited my son, I'm told that my mom snuck a bottle of honey into the neonatal ICU. She kept it hidden deep inside her purse, knowing that, if any of the medical staff caught sight of the bottle, they'd instantly snatch it away. Doctors in the U.S. caution against infants younger than twelve months ingesting honey. Spores in the honey contain bacteria that could get into a newborn's digestive tract, potentially multiplying and producing the toxins for botulism. So the doctors would have accused her of making Ishmael sicker when she knew it was exactly the tonic he needed.

In the neonatal ICU, she gently removed my son from the incubator and held his tiny body pressed to her chest. She waited patiently for the nurse to stop fussing over him and his cords and to leave her alone with her grandson. When at last my mom was sure no one was watching, she whisked the bottle out of her purse. Following the example of the Prophet Muhammad, she recited the opening prayer of the Qur'an in Arabic, *In the name of God, the Entirely Merciful, the Especially Merciful.* As she prayed, she poured a glistening drop of honey onto Ishmael's tongue. Then, feeling his sharp rib bones poking into her soft flesh, she hesitated, thought twice about what she was doing, then poured a second, more generous drop. She relished watching him sucking it down.

Later, she and my dad weren't surprised when, rather than growing sick from botulism, Ismail instead grew so ravenous that he greedily gobbled down bottle after bottle of formula, gaining an astonishing four pounds in less than a week, nearly doubling his birth weight.

This is yet another memory that my brain has tucked away, pretending it's my own.

# 30

By the fourth day in the neuro-ICU, my condition worsened to such an extent that the neurologist pulled Scott aside. It was clear he was in shock. He was busying himself rushing up and down the hospital floors, going up to visit Ishmael, coming back down to visit me, refusing to stop for a moment to make any decisions about proceeding with the EVD, much less about end-of-life care. The neurologist hoped to break through his shock. The pregnancy disease had already taken my life, he told Scott. Even if he didn't make any decisions, it was now just a matter of time. My brain was still not responding to medications. My brain was still swelling. If the pressure in my head continued to build, it would drive my brain downward through the opening of the skull from below, finishing off the process that was well underway.

As a result of having a baby, it appeared I was about to succumb to brain death.

# 31

Living in California these last twenty-five years, I've become acquainted with a growing spirituality that exists outside of organized religions. As I understand it, modern spirituality emphasizes meditation and service to others as a means to discover our true inner path. Suffering mustn't be avoided at all costs. Instead, we should embrace hardships knowing our higher beings attracted the experience as a way to help us evolve into our best selves. The word *surrender* is often used to describe an enlightened state of being—like a palm tree, you should bend easily to the elements, allowing the events of life to blow through you like wind. This idea of surrender is similar in Islamic thought, except that, rather than the higher self, it's God who dispenses hardships as opportunities for spiritual development. The word *Muslim*, as we have come to use it today, refers to the followers of Islam. The Qur'an, however, doesn't make that distinction. It instead states that anyone who believes in one God is a muslim. The word *muslim* is simply one "who has submitted." And the word *islam* is a verb meaning to submit or surrender. As muslims, then, when you bend, you do so in surrender to the Divine.

Both my parents insist that, during the days I was in the neuro-ICU with one foot through death's door, each of them had surrendered. As devout Muslims who'd turned to the story of Abraham in order to bear the unbearable, they each believe that, like the prophet Abraham, they passed an immense test of faith. While this might be true, from what I've gathered over the years, "surrendering" meant something very different to each of my parents. The only times my mom left the hospital were when she went to my house up in the Twin Peaks neighborhood and unfolded the green velvet prayer rug and prostrated. It was in touching her forehead to the ground one evening when things were at their worst that she felt her fears falling away, replaced by a deep sense of peace rising up through her. She knew instantly that my time hadn't come. When she returned to the hospital later that night, she came and stood by my side and, disregarding the life-support machines, told me to ignore the doctors.

To my dad, surrendering meant the opposite. It meant accepting that my time had come. To his mind, there was no other way to explain the chain of events: first, the nine long months when various obstetricians had repeatedly failed to diagnose the eclampsia; then, my labor started on the very night that a bumbling OB happened to be on call and considered himself, regardless of his doctor's oath, too superior to help me; and now, even though I was stationed in the neuro-ICU, finally receiving the care I needed, one of the most advanced medical teams in the world was failing to save me. He was failing to save me, even with all the rituals. For twenty-nine years, from the moment I'd been born under those fateful birth stars, he'd fooled himself into believing that he'd steeled himself for this. Only now did he accept that nothing could have prepared him.

*Miracles*

## 32

According to my medical records, it was during the evening of the fifth day after the delivery that my organs started to switch back on, one after another, like lights in different rooms of a house. My brain began responding to the medication and stopped inflating. Not long after, I emerged from the coma.

To say I woke up to find myself broken would be a lie. My brain wasn't functioning enough to grasp even the most basic facts—I didn't understand that I'd given birth to my son, that I was now stationed in the neuro-ICU ward—so I certainly didn't have the higher mental capacity to gauge what I'd lost.

The day I woke up, Scott leaned into me to say how happy he was. He was crying. I remember watching his eyes tear up. I remember taking in his anguished face. I remember shrinking away from him, frightened.

Mustering up the energy to speak, I whispered, "Who are you?"

# 33

The neurologist must have recognized the faraway look in my eyes.

"Do you know where you are?" he asked, trying to reel me in.

I looked down at my body laid out on the hospital bed, a web of tubes and wires connecting me to machines. I wasn't alarmed. I didn't know to be alarmed. Inside my head, everything had gone silent. No chatter whatsoever, none of the incessant commentary that we're used to. No judgments. At that early stage of recovery, at that late stage of brain trauma, I could only observe the world around me, detached from it. Here were the tubes and wires. Here was a man in a white coat talking to me in a soothing voice. And here was my body. I couldn't put these pieces together to see the larger meaning.

When I didn't answer, the neurologist slowly went over the events, catching me up on everything I'd missed. He told me that I'd successfully delivered my son, that Ishmael was a few floors above me in the nursery, gaining weight and beginning to show signs of thriving, that complications during the delivery had led to transferring me down here.

"You're a lucky woman," he said, remarking that I'd scared the devil out of my family and even, he confided, out of him, something not many patients could do at this point in his career. "I can't take credit for your recovery," he added as though he hoped to clear up some misunderstanding between us. He squeezed my arm gently. "You're our Miracle Girl," he declared.

"Okay," I said. I had no idea what he was talking about.

# 34

*Miracle.*

I've spent a good deal of time considering this word and my relationship to it. Having grown up in a Muslim household and attended Catholic school, the word for me has always been reserved for prophets and scriptures: the parting of the Red Sea, the resurrection of Jesus, Mary's virgin conception. In the New Testament Greek Lexicon, the word often rendered as *miracle* is *semeion*, or "sign." In the Qur'an, the Arabic word *ayah* means a "sign, a miracle or proof." Both traditions understand miracles to be a sign of divine reality.

I can think of only one occasion when it felt appropriate to use this word to describe an incident in my ordinary existence: in my medical files is a second long list of complications alongside my own: meconium, chorioamnionitis, fetal tachycardia with repetitive deep variable decelerations, low Apgar score, infant apnea. When I first read those medical terms, I didn't need to look anything up. I knew instantly what they meant. I could have lost my son.

That he had somehow managed, even as a weakened and malnourished fetus, to fight off the disease and survive was a sign to me of something extraordinary at play.

# 35

While it's true that I didn't recognize Scott, it would be fair to say he didn't recognize me either.

How do I add up the many pieces that were lost to me? And would that then successfully convey how each of these large and small cerebral losses led incrementally to a complete erasure of my being, who I was—or, more accurately, who I thought myself to be—my abilities, my functions, my memories, my dreams, my future? Not only did I not retain a good sense of who I'd been before the damage, but because of the loss of my short-term memory, it was impossible to begin grasping who I'd become. Every moment was instantly forgotten. Every moment was brand-new. Events were sliding away instead of stacking up into some semblance of meaning.

I was also dealing with severe aphasia so I had gaps in my language and could not speak or write what I was experiencing. But even then, I can't rightfully say I was experiencing anything significant, not anymore, not in the way you and I think of experience, as expanding and enriching our lives.

The diffuse brain damage had reduced me to my most primal self. I was no longer a writer and a thinker. I had lost those abilities—not just my words but my higher mental processes to imagine, to plan, to create, to reason, those very functions that we take for granted. Those very functions that are intrinsically human. What I experienced of life was through the narrowest lens possible. I didn't gain insight. I wasn't moved emotionally. I felt no connection to others.

If I had to name one miracle in all this, one saving grace, it would be that my brain damage prevented me from understanding what I'd become. The woman who woke up in the neuro-ICU was not the woman who'd been admitted into labor and delivery. I went into the hospital to have a baby. I came out brain damaged. It's as simple as that. If a comparison of two MRI scans were done right now, one from before the delivery and one from after, you would see an overall shrinkage in my brain. I've taken an intellectual hit. If on the intelligence spectrum I was once average, I am now and will forever remain below that.

# 36

I recognized my family instantly. Since my mom and dad and two brothers have been in my life from its earliest moments, they're stored in the deepest recesses of my brain so, despite the extensive trauma, I knew them right away.

"What are you doing here?" I asked in Urdu when I saw the four crowded around my bed. I had no memory of my three-year estrangement from my dad. No memory that my older brother lived and worked in New York as an investment banker while my younger brother was a neurosurgery resident in Michigan. In my mind, which was drawing on knowledge from my more distant past, it seemed natural that we would all be together, just like when I was growing up. At the same time, a part of me understood that I was somehow separate from them. That they had come to visit me. Was this my home? I looked around at the machines and the wires, the individual nurse's station just outside my space.

Rather than answer me, my dad started praying. He stood with his hands cupped before his chest. He kept shaking his head in astonishment, as though he couldn't believe his eyes.

"We came to see you," my younger brother said, inching closer. I watched him reach out to touch me then, unable to find a spot among the cords and wires, change his mind. He instead turned to my parents. In a quiet tone that he thought I couldn't overhear, he explained that I had short-term memory loss, which was why I asked this question every time they visited. Had they visited before? "It's nothing serious," I heard him comforting my dad in Urdu. Then he switched to English and said to my older brother, "It's common after a coma."

"What are you doing here?" I asked when I opened my eyes and encountered my family huddled around me. I was taken aback by their appearance. My voice came out hoarse and weak, getting lost in the beeping of the machines. I hadn't eaten a bite of food nor had a sip of water for close to a week. Intermittent pneumatic compression devices were wrapped around my lower legs, inflating and deflating every few seconds to prevent a blood clot. And yet it was my family's appearance that genuinely startled me. It seemed to me like they'd suddenly materialized out of thin air.

"We came to see how you're doing, beta," my mom said, inching closer to me.

"Nice," I whispered, not having the strength to say more. I meant that it was nice to see them. My tongue was thick and parched and kept getting stuck to the roof of my mouth. It made a soft clicking noise as it peeled away. There was so much edema inside my body that I wasn't allowed any liquids, not even an ice chip. My mom surprised me by taking my bloated hand into hers. My head felt heavy. I was moving in and out of sleep. Even through my grogginess, I could feel her hunger—all their hunger—to be close to me.

"What are you doing here?" I asked when I woke up next.

## 37

When I was a girl, every year at Christmastime, my family huddled around the TV to watch the 1956 epic film *The Ten Commandments* with Charlton Heston. The Islamic story of Moses is so similar to the Judeo-Christian versions that this movie could have been made for us. It was the only American movie that got my parents to turn off their usual Bollywood VHS tapes. No matter how often we watched *The Ten Commandments* over the years, my parents never tired of witnessing Moses's miracles, how he transformed his staff into a snake and parted the Red Sea. In the Qur'an, Moses is attributed with nine miracles and, similar to what's reported in the Torah, God speaks to Moses near the holy ground of the Burning Bush—after he's asked to remove his sandals, a significant point to my parents since we remove our shoes before stepping onto the sacred ground created by the prayer mat. Watching everything they'd only read about play out on TV in Technicolor delighted my parents to no end. My mom would squeal. My dad would clap his hands at every triumph.

My brothers and I would exchange glances and giggle. We didn't know what was more entertaining, the actors on TV or our parents' reactions.

As a child, the only part in the movie that didn't sit right with me came at the end. I didn't like that the Pharaoh's son dies in the plague. It seemed cruel that Moses didn't bring him back to life. Only now do I understand that bringing someone back to life doesn't mean you haven't lost them.

# 38

One of the reasons the two obstetricians who delivered my son weren't allowed to visit me in the neuro-ICU was because the hospital was worried about a malpractice lawsuit. The way the obstetrician and his senior resident had treated me in the delivery suite, refusing to speak to me, refusing to take my concerns seriously, was a clear violation of their Hippocratic oath. As an important step to becoming doctors, medical students take the oath as a promise to uphold ethical and professional standards while caring for the sick.

Written in Ionic Greek by the ancient physician Hippocrates, the original oath begins: "I swear by Apollo Healer, by Asclepius, by Hygeia, by Panacea, and by all the gods and goddesses, making them my witnesses, that I will carry out, according to my ability and judgment, this oath and this indenture."

Only last year, after I'd realized I could make my way through my thick medical files without the old outrage and sadness, did I look up and read the oath. It was vital that I understand it with a rational mind. Even if those doctors had savagely mistreated me in the delivery suite, then later sent me home from the hospital incapable of caring for myself, incapable of caring for my newborn, while they had simply returned to the labor ward and carried on delivering babies, my hope was that the oath would be a tonic, healing my body of the decades of resentment and disgust. In the end, I never managed to forgive my doctors, but studying the oath did prove restorative in another unexpected way.

Before examining the oath, I hadn't realized that modern medical care has its origins in the ancient Greek world, where healing was connected to religion. The goddesses referenced in the opening lines, Hygeia and Panacea, recognizable in the words *hygiene* and *panacea*, are both goddesses of healing. Asclepius is the Greek god of medicine. The first hospitals in Western civilization were located in Greece. Called the Asclepieia, these hospitals were really sanctuaries and sacred temples of worship of the healer god Asclepius. But not all ailing people were welcome. While the ill were treated with sacred respect, according to written sources, the Temple of Asclepius was considered to be so holy that only those who'd been invited by the priests could make the pilgrimage. Miracles were known to occur there. Incurable diseases were cured. Paraplegics were made to walk. A blind man whose eyes were so damaged that he had nothing but eyelids was given sight. A little boy who couldn't speak was granted speech. A woman named Kleo who'd been pregnant for five years finally gave birth to a boy after visiting the temple. Her newborn emerged from her belly as a four-year-old and proceeded to wash himself and follow his mother around the temple grounds.

Growing up in the U.S., I'd learned to separate science from faith. But intrinsic to the Hippocratic Oath are both medicine and prayer, which, when combined, result in miraculous healings. From those days I was in a coma, one of the only memories I've retained is of my mom whispering in my ear. Sheep were being sacrificed. An imam was charging to the summit of a mountain. These past decades, I often wondered why I'd grown alert right then, to hear her terrifying words of comfort. Here, finally, rising out of the ancient Greek world, might have been the answer.

# 39

My body was an ocean. My organs were floating islands. And yet I'd never been so thirsty in my life. When my friend Naomi visited me, I convinced her to go out and bring me back a fruit smoothie.

"Not a kid-size smoothie," I croaked, my tongue thick and floppy in my mouth. "The largest you can find."

She was scandalized. "Honey, you're under strict orders: absolutely no liquids! You heard the neurologist, you're lucky to be alive."

"I'm allowed to drink whatever I want," I said firmly. "And I want the largest fruit smoothie you can buy."

"What? I haven't heard that. Are you sure the doctors say it's okay?"

"I promise."

Desperate to do something for me, Naomi left the hospital and walked down the hill to 9th Ave in the Inner Sunset neighborhood and ordered me a large smoothie at Jamba Juice. Within minutes, she was at my bedside again. Just as she was handing me the sixteen-ounce cup, my private nurse snatched the smoothie away and tossed it into the garbage.

In Naomi's telling of this episode, I sound articulate, even aware enough of my restrictions to cleverly find a way around them. But in my memories of those early days, I'm nothing like this. I'm lethargic and disoriented. Stunned neurons are flickering on and off. Once, when the neurologist entered my cubicle with a long line of residents behind him, I started giggling and poked fun at them all for showing up with hot-pink hair. My vision wasn't functioning. I called them clowns. Several of the residents backed away. They were young and inexperienced and couldn't hide their alarm. At the same time, my damaged brain zeroed in on heightened emotions like a vicious, pouncing animal. Their fear of me made me laugh louder. That's the person I remember, the one who had no awareness of her distorted reality. So I know that when I assured Naomi that I was allowed to drink whatever I wanted, I wasn't lying.

To this day Naomi jokes that, after everything I'd survived, she could have killed me with a tall cup of juice. Whenever I hear her say this, I know what she really means. Deeply spiritual and intuitive, my dear friend believes there's a reason that nurse appeared out of nowhere just in the nick of time.

## 40

Word got around. A slew of doctors I'd never met before, doctors who'd only heard rumors about the Miracle Girl, went out of
their way to track me down behind the locked double doors of the
neuro-ICU. They stormed into my curtained space with clip-
boards and pens. They urged me to grant them permission to write
scientific papers about me. They wanted to present these papers
at medical conferences. They were exhilarated, lit up by some sort
of electricity humming through their body. They were in awe. They
jammed their pens into my hand. They showed me where to sign
my name at the bottom of legal documents, granting permission.
With great authority, they grabbed my thick medical chart and
paged through it, exclaiming and muttering to themselves.

"No," Scott said, shooing away doctor after doctor, chasing
them out of the cramped space.

"No," I began saying whenever an unfamiliar doctor
stopped by. What was I saying no to? Who knew? I was just
having fun imitating Scott like a toddler imitates adults
when first learning to speak.

# 41

For once, my parents were in agreement with the doctors.

When the two were at my bedside talking quietly to each other, thinking I was asleep, I heard them repeatedly using the Urdu word *mojiza*, miracle.

Our relatives in India had been informed of the *mojiza*, and so had my parents' close Muslim friends in Minneapolis. The imam came back down the mountain. Sheep were spared from slaughter. Mutton biryani was no longer served at orphanages. And then, after a day's pause, it started up once more. Two more sheep were sacrificed. Orphans were fed. The imam carried the Qur'an up to the summit and sat reciting it from cover to cover. Except now, it was all being done to express my parents' gratitude to Allah for this *mojiza*.

# 42

When I was first learning to read the Qur'an at six years old, my tutor in Hyderabad required that I keep my left hand on the table between us during the session. This made it easy for him to strike my wrist with a wooden ruler at every mispronunciation, which occurred so often that I remember once peeing my pants just so I could skip the day's lesson. While my first language, Urdu, utilizes the Arabic alphabet, the two share very few words—and even those words have slight variations. The Urdu word for book, *kitab*, is *kitaabun* in Arabic. I say *kursi* for chair, but it's *kursiun* in Arabic. Each of the twenty-eight Arabic letters represents a hard consonant and, unlike Urdu, diacritical marks like short dashes are used to clarify vowel sounds. What made the Qur'an even more difficult to read as a child is its highly stylized calligraphy. Individual letters merge and run together as they do in English cursive, but in Arabic, an entire letter could be whittled down to a mere squiggle and a dot and I'd have to be able to decipher and differentiate. I usually ended the tutoring sessions with a raw and bruised hand.

These lessons took place in the drawing room of my dad's grand house in the Old City, which was the formal sitting area set aside for male visitors unrelated to the family. The drawing room was designed with two doors, one leading further inside the house and the other directly outside. For several summer months every year, the same tutor came to teach my older brother and me and, in all that time, he never once set foot inside the main house. He never once set eyes on my mom. The only woman who could come and go into the drawing room as she pleased, even without a head covering, was my ayah, Fiza. As a servant, she had more freedoms than my mother. But those freedoms were a sign of her working-class status. So it was she who would bring my tutor chai and biscuits, relay any messages to my mom about my progress, and also pass along the weekly tutoring fees.

During our sessions, my tutor sat across a table from me, eyes lowered because it was improper for him to look directly at me. Even though I was just a little girl, I was still a female. He didn't keep a copy of the Qur'an open on his side of the table to follow along as I recited. He didn't need to. He had the entire book memorized. Once, while I was clumsily making my way through a verse, doing my best to read the Arabic script from right to left, my ayah stepped into the room to serve him chai. In shifting my copy of the Qur'an to allow space for the teacup, I lost my place and bungled the pronunciation of a word. Before I had a chance to correct myself, he reached across with the ruler. Just as it came down, I snapped my hand back and we both heard a loud cracking noise as it struck the table. He was infuriated and demanded that I place my hand back on the table. I refused. The back of my hand was already turning purple, the skin was cracking open, and I couldn't bear another hit. I turned to Fiza for help. She had always protected me, even when it meant standing up to my mother, so I was surprised to see her hesitate. But as she took in my pleading face, she started to mumble something to my tutor, who instantly shut her up.

"The child must learn to respect the Word," he said.

Fiza stood absolutely still as she considered what he'd said. Then she carefully took my left hand into hers. "Stop rushing," she advised as she gently massaged it before placing my hand back on the table. "Hold each letter in your mouth and ear."

Before I could register what she was doing, the ruler struck my wrist so severely that the pain reverberated all the way up to my elbow. My eyes instantly filled with tears. Fiza clucked her tongue as she tried to rub the pain away. After that, every time I went into a tutoring session, I felt so vulnerable that I stumbled even more over the Arabic, my gaze darting repeatedly to the ruler.

"Child!" my tutor finally snapped one afternoon at the end of his patience. "Our Prophet, peace be upon him, was illiterate when the angel appeared and commanded him to recite. This is not any ordinary book. You are reading God's words. Show some respect!"

The way my parents explained it to me, the Prophet had to be illiterate just as Mary had to be a virgin. Pure, divine vessels. The Qur'an is thought to be Muhammed's only miracle as a prophet. The reason my ayah couldn't stand up for me when

I was being punished, and the reason my tutor demanded correct pronunciation was because Muslims believe that God authored the book, sending it down chapter by chapter over twenty-three years with the angel Gabriel. In the centuries since, not a letter has been altered by human hands. Everything about the text is considered sacred, every word and every letter, including the exact arrangement of those words and letters, and the sound they create when recited. As a child, holding a copy of the Qur'an made me feel like Moses in the movie *The Ten Commandments*, clutching the tablets God had just emblazoned with divine law. Am I worthy of touching this? What if I drop it? There are rules in place for properly handling the holy book. I always remove my shoes before nearing the Qur'an and cover my head with a scarf.

But the rules don't apply only to the Qur'an. Since God is associated with the written word, I was taught that all books and writing tools are sacred, as are those things that they beget: knowledge, the act of learning, the art of verse, and the art of calligraphy. If I dropped a book or a pen on the ground or, worse, if I then accidentally stepped on or grazed it with my foot, it was considered a high offense to God. I would have to pick up the book or pen immediately and bring it to my face, place the object against my right eye and then against my left eye, then press it to my lips with a kiss to show my respect. When I started writing myself, I saw the act as akin to prayer. Equally, then, losing my ability to speak due to severe aphasia, and losing my higher powers to think and conceptualize, demonstrated the opposite of the miracle everyone was heralding. It was God withdrawing from my life.

# 43

The only one who refrained from saying that my recovery was a miracle was Scott. As an atheist, he didn't believe in miracles. Grown tired of hearing the word thrown about, he began correcting people by pointing to the equipment and machines in the room.

In the months before I'd gotten pregnant, Scott had lost both his parents in quick succession, his mom from lung cancer and then his dad from a massive heart attack. Rather than a church service, he held a celebration of life. There were no burials, only cremations and a scattering of the ashes in the Pacific. A short time after their deaths, when I discovered I was pregnant, I immediately thought of his mom, who'd wished desperately to live long enough to meet her first grandchild.

"Maybe she's looking down at us right now," I told Scott, but I was really consoling myself.

"You mean, *from heaven*?" he asked in a mocking tone. Scott was almost nihilistic in his views. The afterlife, heaven and hell, angels, God: these were fairy tales meant to give life purpose. He rejected the idea that life had to have meaning. "We are born and we die," he'd said on each occasion we'd scattered his parents' ashes. "From nothing to nothing."

To me, it seemed inconceivable that the trajectory of an entire lifetime boiled down to a point of emptiness. As naive as he supposed me to be, I had to believe in a higher intelligence, no matter what name you gave you it. Visualizing myself dissolving into a black void bled out the magic of existence. Why even go on? While I could accept his refusal to buy into religious allegories, his insistence that "this was it" seemed a superficial approach that stripped the world of its complexity, and so made me question why he even became a poet. A writer's job was sacred. Rumi, Rilke, Wordsworth, Plath, Rabia—from east and west, all uncovered hidden truths, capturing the extraordinary secrets of an ordinary moment. A poet's verses gave us hope and direction and insights, not only through the nuances of language but also in what was left unsaid, the silence between each word and line. Narrative informed our lives, from the stories passed down to us to the stories we told ourselves, so his attitude sometimes left me feeling alienated from him. That I married Scott in spite of such a deep philosophical difference simply affirmed what I felt I already knew: that love is extraordinarily powerful.

But when I was in the hospital, listening to him scoff at the term "Miracle Girl," none of these usual thoughts were triggered. My memory of Scott and our history were wiped clean.

# 44

"Think of your brain as a puzzle," the neurologist was telling me. We'd just finished another round of his poking and prodding. Can you move your toes? Can you grip my fingers firmly? Your eye is droopy. Can you tell me how many fingers I'm holding up? You're gripping your chest—on a scale of 1 to 10, how would you rate the pain? You're not getting enough oxygen; you need to exercise your lungs by breathing deeper. It was late. He was on his way home. My parents had already left for the night. Scott was up in the room he'd been assigned on the maternity ward eating a hospital dinner. My private nurse was switching shifts. The latest MRI scan results had just come back and it was clear that something about them had disturbed the neurologist. He spoke slowly and intentionally, watching my face for any signs of understanding.

"In a healthy brain all the pieces fit together. The connections between brain cells are called neural pathways. Those pathways keep everything running smoothly." To illustrate this, he interlaced his fingers, locking his two hands together. "The global trauma to your brain has scattered those pieces." He pulled his hands apart and held up all ten fingers for me to see, splayed apart. "Your job from here on out is to recover as many puzzle pieces as possible to put yourself back together."

I was too debilitated to understand what he was telling me, and I remember looking as intently into his face as he was mine, searching for clues from his expression. Despite the concern I detected in his voice, he kept his face emotionless, perhaps intentionally so as not to alarm me.

He must have seen my confusion because he finally patted my arm and said, "You know what? I think tomorrow might be a great day for you to meet your son!" As the new nurse slipped inside the curtain carrying a needle for yet another blood draw, the neurologist told her, "Let's get Ishmael down here tomorrow. Meeting him might be the spark Mom here needs."

## 45

In preparation for meeting my newborn, my nurse adjusted my bed so that I was in a seated position. Then she adjusted my arms, explaining how I was to hold my son. Finally, the neonatal nurse wheeled my newborn down from the nursery to the neuro-ICU in an incubator. She gently broke the news to me that he'd been stationed in the neonatal ICU since the delivery, but I didn't ask what was wrong with him. She told me that his health was frail and she didn't like bringing him down to this ward, that the visit would be kept short to ensure he wasn't exposed to bacteria. Again, I didn't say anything. I simply watched the nurse carefully open the incubator and gently set his little body in my arms. I held him exactly as my nurse had instructed.

My mom and dad, Scott and the two nurses, all held their breath in anticipation. I could feel their excitement. It alerted me that this was a pivotal meeting, that I should be feeling something momentous myself. But I had lost my depth perception and had blotches in my vision, blind spots preventing me from seeing the entirety of what was in front of me—similar to looking at a photograph where insects have eaten away holes. My body was weakened from the many days I'd lain limp in bed as well as by my many injuries. A plastic pump was pushing oxygen into my nostrils. And I was dimly confused and lethargic.

Still, I clutched my newborn as best I could and closed one eye and shifted my head about, thinking I could somehow maneuver to see beyond the splotches. No matter what I tried, I couldn't get a good look at my son. A round gray spot in my vision shifted with my movements, blocking out his features. I grew frustrated. My arms were on fire. At six pounds my son's weight was too much for me to bear. His hard skull was pressing down on needles shooting into my veins. I fumbled over words, trying to tell the nurse to take him from me. Not understanding what I was saying, she smiled indulgently. Why in the world was my family still gawking at me? I grunted in pain. Then I made a decision that seemed perfectly reasonable at the time but haunts me still today. Unable to endure the agony any longer, I simply let go of my son. His little body fell awkwardly across my lap. I heard a faint sound like a hiccup followed by a loud shriek. The nurse swooped forward and scooped him up. Scott and my parents crowded around her, patting my son's back, soothing him. I watched them glancing at one another, speechless, horrified.

I felt nothing but relief.

# 46

The first time I understood something was wrong with me was when my dad began arguing with one of the doctors who came in to perform a routine neurological exam. This neurologist happened to be of Indian descent, and my dad, upon seeing another Indian face, immediately launched into complaints about my care. He told her that he'd understand if I'd fallen through the cracks at a hospital in India but not at a hospital of this caliber!

From the argument, I gathered that my dad had been demanding that the hospital let him meet with the obstetrician who'd delivered my baby, the tall, wiry man with an Australian accent. No matter how often he'd insisted, that obstetrician never showed his face. Why was it that he was never among the long line of doctors who came to see me every day, my dad wanted to know. The OB's absence became a point of contention, angering my dad to the point where he became intent on suing the hospital.

"Have you seen what's become of my daughter?" he now

asked the neurologist, incensed. "She's twenty-nine. She came here to have a baby. Now look at her! Don't you think the very least that doctor can do is come and take a good look at her to see what he's done?" He was shaking with anger.

"What do you mean 'take a look at me,' Daddy?" I asked him in Urdu, confused by what he was saying about me and frightened by his rage. Just as with a newborn's brain, just as with my son's brain, in those early days, it was intense emotions like these that cut through to make an impression. Hearing the fury in my dad's voice, I shrank into myself in my hospital bed. Up until then, the brain damage had served as a sort of blessing: my lack of comprehension shielded me from being able to perceive what I'd become. Although I now recognized something had changed in me, I couldn't see what exactly that might be. But I could sense from my dad's heightened emotions that it wasn't good.

When my dad didn't answer straight away, I asked quietly again, "What happened to me, Daddy?"

Since Urdu is my first language, it's hardwired in the Broca's area of my brain and so was left intact. English, which I'd learned in grade school, was difficult for me now. The French I'd learned in high school and had become fluent in, as well as the Arabic I'd been tutored in as a child and then formally studied in college, had vanished. The only Arabic I retained was in the form of prayers I'd memorized as a child. Although I had no trouble communicating in Urdu, I must have regressed to sounding like a toddler because my mother immediately stepped in and spoke to me in the same high-pitched tone that I'd heard her using with my newborn.

"Nothing happened to you, beta," she consoled me. "You made it through, didn't you? The only thing that's happened is a *mojiza*."

She swatted my dad's arm and ordered him to control himself.

Not grasping the larger nuances of what was taking place around me, I believed her. And so it was that all my development over the years, my learning and my knowledge and my artistic expression, evaporated along with the dead neurons, and I was once more a child, needing my parents to explain the world to me, to care for and comfort me, to assure me that I was going to be just fine.

# 47

On the day Scott informed me that there was nothing more the doctors could do, that he was finally able to take me home, I immediately lunged at him, casting my body over the metal side rails of my bed and pushing him away with as much might as I could muster.

"Nooo!" I cried, throwing a tantrum. My voice echoed off the walls and reverberated through the quiet unit, making me feel stronger than I was. "No, no, no, no husband!" I shouted. My anger cut my words short. There was so much more I wanted to say, but the words wouldn't form in my mouth. Home? I had no memory of my house up in the Twin Peaks neighborhood. And I didn't have the capacity to imagine a world outside my curtained room in the neuro-ICU. But it was no use. Three days after I emerged from the coma, I was transferred back up to the fifteenth and top floor of the hospital and moved into the recovery room where Scott had been staying, and where, if things had gone differently, I would have landed right after the delivery. The room was saturated with the sweet scent of flowers. Countless bouquets had been sent by relatives and friends from around the country, expressing concerns over my complications, expressing joy over my son's birth. There was no space left to set the vases and some were even tucked into the corners of the floor where no one could knock them over.

The labor and delivery ward was loud and animated. People were laughing. Babies crying. Nurses spoke boisterously to one another in the hallways. It was in sharp contrast to the enforced silence I'd grown used to and even required in order to heal from the cerebral trauma. The bright colors of the flowers, the overpowering scent, the laughter, and the high-spirited energy reverberating around me—my brain was overwhelmed by the stimulation. I didn't know how to understand this sudden expansion of my world. Of the four nights I spent in this ward, I remember mostly wishing to return to the neuro-ICU. My head hurt and I needed sleep, but the nurses woke me every three hours to untie my hospital gown and position my son's body across my bare chest. Then they sat on the bed next to me and patiently waited to see if his suckling would produce milk. On top of everything I'd suffered, now I had to endure raw and bleeding nipples. The nurses were following procedure, didn't seem to understand what I now know: that my body wasn't able to nurture another life when it had to first ensure my survival.

Nearly two weeks after my son was born, my parents and my brothers and Scott arrived together to bring my son and me home. I still didn't understand where I was being taken so when my neurologist stopped by to say goodbye, I latched on to his arm and begged to return to my quiet cubicle. My head was pounding. But the neurologist assured me that the familiar setting of our home would not only help trigger memories but would also accelerate my recovery.

"You've made a remarkable recovery," he told me. And for the first time since he'd taken over my care, I thought I saw him smile. Minutes later, however, he took Scott aside and cautioned him to be patient with me. "The woman you brought to the hospital," he told Scott in his usual soft tones, "is not the woman you're bringing home." He explained that the first six months would be vital to my recovery. Motor skills tended to return first. But, he warned Scott, the higher processes of the mind, the processes we use to think and imagine and plan and reason—those processes that separate us from animals—well, he wasn't confident when those would return, if ever.

The grim prognosis did nothing to dampen Scott's spirits. He seemed to have grown used to hearing pessimistic news. He thanked the neurologist for everything he'd done then turned to me grinning from ear to ear.

"Going home," he whispered.

There was something about the lively ward that relaxed my family. Scott began shooting pictures to mark the day. Ishmael was lying in an isolette next to my bed, wrapped in a white cotton blanket printed with a wide, blue stripe. I noticed he had gray-blue eyes with wisps of blond lashes and brows. It was the first time I had seen my son awake.

My older brother brought Ishmael a stuffed gray elephant and was using it to play peekaboo with him. My younger brother kept exclaiming how lucky I was to be going home.

"I have to admit, I had my doubts," he kept saying, first to me in English, then to my parents in Urdu.

"*Alhamdulillah*," my mom and dad answered together, giving thanks to God.

A nurse I didn't recognize came into the room and began filling a brown paper bag full of items the hospital was sending home with me: a package of very large menstrual pads, newborn diapers, a manual breast pump, a manual spirometer that I was instructed to blow into multiple times a day in order to regain my lung capacity and pump more oxygen to my heart, as well as a strange combination of medications, which among others was metoprolol for my high blood pressure and heart attack, barbiturates to lower intracranial pressure, and a stool softener because I'd received a third-degree perineal laceration to accommodate the forceps delivery. As she packed my items, she flirted with Scott and my older brother. She told them that the nurses had been admiring Ishmael's long fingers and were betting that he'd grow up to be either a pianist or a surgeon.

"You'll have to stay in touch so we know how it all turns out," she teased, lightly touching Scott's arm.

The exertion to process all this stimulation quickly exhausted me. The wires in my brain blew a fuse. I started mistaking my son for his new stuffed animal. Even though my eyes could plainly see Ishmael, my brain was convinced that there was a tiny gray elephant wrapped in the white cotton blanket instead of a baby.

While I was trying to work this out, my younger brother pulled up a chair next to my bed. He spoke slowly to me, quietly, as he might speak to one of his patients, as my own neurologist had routinely spoken to me down in the neuro-ICU. The familiarity of the tone caught my attention. It was exactly what I needed to calm my nerves and help ease me into this noisy, chaotic world that everyone else seemed to take for granted.

"This isn't going to be like recovering from the flu, you know," he cautioned me. "There's no road map here. You don't just gradually get better." He went on to say that he'd already explained all this to Scott and to our parents too. He wanted everyone to have realistic expectations. Recovery wasn't going to be a linear process. Since neurons don't regenerate, I had to create new neural pathways. And creating those new neural pathways was going to be a tedious and exhausting task of repeating basic functions over and again—taking a step and another, and another, saying one word in English and then another, and another. "No more miracles," he said, chuckling. Just tiresome, repetitive motions that would help to rewire my brain, and that new wiring would then help me to overcome my deficits—not by regaining what I'd lost but by relearning those tasks and functions. "You and Ishmael are kind of on the same journey," he was saying. "You won't suddenly remember how to do things. You're going to have to learn everything all over again, kinda like you did when we were little. Maybe you can use Ishmael as inspiration, you know. Maybe he can be your road map?"

# PART TWO

When I let go of what I am,
I become what I might be.

—LAO TZU

# Hungry Ghosts

# 48

The urge to buy a house overtook me in the early weeks of my pregnancy. Up until then, Scott and I had been content renting and hadn't given much thought to where we might eventually settle down. Two years earlier, we'd graduated from our writing program in the Pacific Northwest and had decided to skip the graduation ceremony to move to San Francisco. His mother had just been diagnosed with fourth-stage lung cancer so we felt an urgency to be nearby. We leased a large one-bedroom flat on Ashbury Street perched on a hill with views of Golden Gate Park and the ocean. Every morning, Scott made the one-hour commute down I-280 to teach at Stanford. After his last afternoon class, he drove along Palm Drive to his parents' home in Palo Alto off University Avenue to check in on his mom, whose health was quickly declining. After dinner with his parents, he'd trek back up to our apartment in the city, where he'd sit late into the night grading student papers and writing. His poetry during this time spoke of the lengthy solitary treks he'd taken during his college and graduate years through far-flung countries. One described him sitting alone on the banks of the Ganges along the ghats of Varanasi watching dead bodies burning in the funeral pyres.

While he was away for long hours, I tried to get my first novel off the ground. Part of the reason I'd felt justified in skipping the graduation ceremony was because the writing program had not only failed my expectations but, worse, had proven to be toxic. Professors were ill-suited to teaching the craft of fiction and instead belittled students. On the last day of classes, the director of the program, who'd initially recruited me, even granting me a full ride based on the merits of my writing, pulled me into his office to let me know that I'd been the worst mistake he'd ever made. You'll never get published, he'd pronounced, staring me down from across his large desk. His words followed me down the Pacific Coast and into our one-bedroom apartment in San Francisco and hung over me as I sat alone for hours. His voice jeered at every hesitant word I typed. In a moment of rage, I deleted everything I'd written during the two years of graduate school. I then created a new file. But there, on the empty screen, was his smug face peering out at me. The only way through the writer's block was not by trying to ignore him, I realized, but by proving him wrong. In fits and starts, I amassed forty crisp opening pages to a new manuscript. It was Scott who urged me to send them out to agents. When I refused, worried that any rejection would stall me again, he gave the pages to a former professor of his at Berkeley, who, in turn, dispatched them to her agency in New York. Within a week, a literary contract arrived at our apartment by FedEx. A year later, I was in the midst of finishing the book to send off to my agent when I discovered I was pregnant. A baby, a literary contract, a supportive and loving husband who'd grown up locally: there was no reason not to settle down. And there was also this: I wanted to give my son the grounding I never had as a child being shuttled between two home countries.

Just as I was entering my second trimester, we purchased a house nestled in the hills of the Twin Peaks neighborhood. A 1909 Victorian had been gutted to create sunlit open spaces. While the front rooms had views of the Bay Bridge, the two bedrooms were toward the rear, the master opening onto a garden with a red brick patio. Scott and I looked forward to our son playing in that garden while we sat under the magnolia tree, reading and laughing together. In the nursery, Scott assembled a crib. Together, we invested in two custom-built bookcases with glass doors to hold the large collection of books we'd amassed over the years—poetry and short story anthologies, novels, plays, philosophy and post-colonial theory, Qur'anic analyses, Buddhist thought—and to those we now added board books: *Are You My Mother?*, *Goodnight Moon*, *Go Dog. Go!* After the five-month sonogram confirmed I was having a boy, I went shopping with Naomi and bought the tiniest article of clothing I'd ever held in my hands: a cotton one-piece with covered feet, printed with black-and-gold-striped zebras. I packed it in the overnight hospital bag for Ishmael to wear home. Scott carefully framed and placed bright watercolors that his mom, a talented artist who'd sadly succumbed to cancer earlier that year, had painted. Across the wooden floors, I spread thick, handwoven wool rugs I'd picked up in Kashmir. Scott upholstered an armchair with an indigo blue shibori fabric he'd brought back from his two years of living and teaching in Tokyo. In one corner of the master bedroom, looking out at the peaceful back garden, was my writing desk and laptop with a half-completed manuscript of my novel.

After the delivery, when I arrived home from the hospital and my two brothers helped me up the front stoop and into the living room with its breathtaking views and bright watercolors displayed on the walls and a library of books inside glass doors, it was like walking into a stranger's home. I recognized nothing. When the two then slowly walked me to my bedroom and helped me under the covers, it was no different than being transferred to the maternity ward from the neuro-ICU, from one bed to another. It never crossed my mind to check to see if Ishmael was dressed in the little outfit with the black-and-gold-striped zebras. I suppose this is what spiritual traditions mean when they stress nonattachment. It's a state I tried to reach when I couldn't stop hearing the MFA director's condemnation of me and ended up walking down the street to a Buddhist center and registering for meditation classes. By disengaging from my emotions and ties and memories and worldly concerns, including any attachment to future outcomes, I was able to find a way through my fears and begin writing. Now I understand that when you are truly detached from everything around you, when it is not something you're trying to achieve but a true state of being, it is a cold and isolating feeling.

# 49

While my newborn slept for long hours in his nursery, I took
possession of the back bedroom of the house. There, with
the curtains closed against the sunlight, I slept long, and I
slept undisturbed in a way that I hadn't been able to in the
hospital with the nurses constantly waking me, and I slept
drugged to the hilt on barbiturates. Soon enough the hands
on the clock lost all meaning. The hours of the day no longer
determined my schedule, the needs of my body did. Like my
son, I woke when I was hungry or when I had to use the toilet.
The minute the needs of my body were met, I was out like a
light. There were moments during my convalescence when I
was vaguely aware of the happenings around me, moments
when snippets of conversation floated back to the bedroom
or laughter when friends stopped by with a meal, everyone
eating together while passing Ishmael around. But none of
this activity seeped into my dreams. Dreams are stories that
our brain, disconnected from the environment, creates to
give meaning to random nerve signals, so I wasn't capable

of dreaming back then. I was submerged inside a great still-ness. Weeks collapsed into a single day. A single day with-ered down into a single hour, a lone minute, then vanished altogether.

# 50

While I slept as deeply as my newborn those first two weeks, my family began to return to their lives. My older brother flew back to his job in New York. My younger brother went back to Michigan to resume his neurosurgery residency. My dad returned home to Minneapolis. Naomi resumed teaching at Harvard. Scott began his commute down to Stanford. Every morning before he left, he checked in on me, smelling fresh from the shower. He always came holding Ishmael. He refrained from getting too near, knowing I'd push him away. Instead, he sat across the room, behind my desk, in my writing chair. Once settled, he'd nurse our son on formula while he filled me in on the latest happenings. I was sleepy and listless and impaired, so only caught snippets. Now that he'd returned to work, he had weeks of catching up to do, armloads of rhetoric essays to grade. After exhausting days on campus, he spent evenings with our son, reading to him from board books we'd bought together, nursing him, then letting him nap on his chest while he graded student essays.

He was so scared of accidentally hitting my head in his sleep that he decided it was best for him to sleep on the sofa.

"Not that you'd welcome me in the bed anyway," he once joked.

Because I kept forgetting, he had to repeatedly remind me that my brothers and my dad and Naomi had left, but that my mom had graciously stayed on to help. Scott had moved our son's brand-new crib out of the nursery, dismantled it, and stored it in the garage. He purchased a double bed and set it up in the nursery, turning it into a guest bedroom for my mom. In the closet and dresser drawers, next to where I'd placed Ishmael's baby clothes—gifts I'd received at my baby shower, hand-me-downs from my friend Naomi, whose child was now one year old, cute onesies I'd purchased and was looking forward to dressing Ishmael in—my mom added her own clothes, loose cotton tunics and *shalwar* pants that she could comfortably wear as she dove into the responsibilities of caring for my newborn and me. Still shaken that Ishmael had stopped breathing and landed in the neonatal ICU, she slept with my son snuggled up against her on the double bed, just as she'd done with me when my parents first immigrated to Minneapolis and we slept as a family on one queen bed—me pressed up against my mom's stomach and my older brother pressed up against her back, my dad nearly falling off the mattress. At all hours of the night, she'd wake to place a palm lightly on Ishmael's chest, checking for its delicate rise and fall—*was it from Scott or from my mom that I learned these details?* Who was sitting in my chair nursing Ishmael and talking to me? I was so woozy, I couldn't tell when one left and the other entered. Every morning, after changing him out of his soiled pajamas and diaper, she bathed him in the kitchen sink and brushed his gums with her index finger. At a time when I was nearly as helpless as my newborn, my mom slipped into the role of a new mother.

"Your dad and I consulted an imam," she once announced. "Ismail was born under the most auspicious birth stars. What a relief not to have that hanging over me!"

## 51

A part of me began observing Ishmael carefully, detecting the slightest development: at nearly a month old, he was able to bring his hands to his mouth and suck on his fists, his eyes were following the light, his head automatically turned toward sound, his legs were constantly kicking. But witnessing these milestones didn't bring me joy. I wasn't looking at him with the nurturing gaze of a new mom. Our rhythms were lining up. That was what some part of me was taking note of. More and more now, he and I seemed to be sleeping and waking and eating at about the same times.

On certain days, when I awoke groggier than usual and my head felt like it was about to crack and I had to beg my mom to press down on my skull with her two fists to apply counterpressure, that part of me that was noticing our parallel development zeroed in on my son. My survival instinct was on overdrive. Of the many family members and friends who'd gathered around me during that era, my son was the one who most threatened my well-being. In my mind, he and I were competing for my mom's care. If I asked my mom to massage my throbbing head and she put me off because she was feeding him or if she delayed in giving me my pain medications or helping me to the bathroom because he was taking up her attention that same minute, I'd fall deep into a primal rage, raw and wild and uncontrollable.

"You're *my* mom," I once snarled at her so violently that the menace in my voice stopped her in her tracks. Maternal instincts are not innate, I discovered. Giving birth doesn't automatically transform a woman into a caregiver. The urge to protect, the urge to nurture, the urge to die in the place of your child, if the situation so demands: these instincts arise from love and love arises from a bond. And I felt no bond with my son. My mom stared at me for a full minute as though she didn't know who I was, taking in my face, the murderous look in my eyes. I noticed that for the rest of that day, she didn't bring my son anywhere near me.

The best way to describe the lack of connection I felt to my son is to recall how I felt when Scott sometimes sat in my desk chair with Ishmael on his lap and read out loud to me from baby development books. It was his way of both involving me as a parent and also reassuring himself that he wasn't parenting alone. *At the end of three months*, he'd read, *he'll be able to lift his head and shoulders. At seven months, he'll be sitting on his own. At twelve to thirteen months, he'll be taking his first step.* I was once a writer—Scott was still a writer and he mistakenly believed that words would continue to have the same impact on me as before: dissolving distances between worlds, transcending barriers, bringing us together in our shared humanity.

But when I listened to his words and tried to imagine what my son might be like in one year, in one month, tomorrow, rather than envisioning some future incarnation of Ishmael, I instead came face-to-face with a blank screen. The higher functions to project a future had blinked out. So it was like staring at the gray image a Polaroid camera spits out . . . except that the grayness never dissipates to reveal the captured image below.

# 52

There was a problem with being the Miracle Girl.

And that problem became more apparent as the days and weeks and months went by. No one wanted to take responsibility for my recovery. When I woke from the coma in the neuro-ICU, the neurologist had made it clear that he had fully expected my body to succumb to multiple organ failure and global ischemia. He had no medical explanation for how it was possible that I was still here. When I was discharged from the hospital, a doctor from every department whose care I was under came to see me off, summarizing my case through the lens of their specialty—my heart, my blood, my liver, my kidneys, my lungs, my brain—and yet not one of them, not even the neurologist, thought to give me a referral to a physical or speech therapist. When I think back on it, the omission is so outrageous that I have to presume the doctors had washed their hands of me. They were taking a wait-and-see approach: wait a year for my brain to shrink back down to normal size, then see which deficits I had to learn to live with permanently.

It was like they'd passed on my medical care to whatever invisible power they credited for intervening and keeping me alive. Or they'd passed it on to my mom and husband, who were doing their best to care for me, but who didn't have the medical background I needed. Or, more likely, they'd simply left it up to me, a brain-damaged mother with a newborn, to find a way to heal myself.

# 53

Every summer we landed back in Hyderabad, my mom took me to a faith healer for what I can only describe as an annual checkup. Endlessly tormented by the tragedy foretold by my birth stars, she turned to healers to protect me as much as she could. For those living in the ancient alleyways of the Old City, it was commonplace to see evil apparitions and ghosts and demons and jinns walking the dirt streets as clearly as they saw their neighbors. The trick to distinguishing between a flesh-and-blood human and an evil spirit was to look at the feet. If the soles were turned upside down, facing upward, then you were encountering a *shaytan*. Superstitions ran rampant with ways to keep yourself free of possession: don't stand under trees with untied hair. Don't toss fingernail clippings without first spitting on them. Thoroughly clean combs and brushes of stray strands then burn the hair. Don't ever leave shoes turned upside down, ready to be slipped into by the devil, who would then slip inside you. Since the human body wasn't sealed and protected, as it might look to us with the naked eye, it was accepted that anything could possess the body at any moment, if you weren't careful. So, together, my mom and I would sit cross-legged on the ground in front of the spiritual healer, knowing that a good exorcism would rid me of any foul energies that might have latched on since my last visit, ready to cause harm.

The last healer I went to with my mom was when I was eighteen, and she and my dad were both convinced I was possessed by a lecherous, hungry ghost. It was the only way they could explain why, three days before I was to get married, I was refusing to go through with it. Hungry ghosts are demon-like creatures that were once living people but whose sins have damned them to a tormented and cursed in-between existence, unable to fully die, unable to come back to life. Filled with rage and insatiable desires, they can latch on to the living, sucking their life energy and driving them insane. Because I wouldn't move forward and do what my parents felt was in my best interests and get married, they believed some lustful ghost must have been behind my erratic behavior.

I tried to tell my parents that, in fact, I'd been refusing the match for ten whole months, ever since they finalized the marriage with the suitor's parents without consulting me. But they continued to disregard my protests. My dad's eyes turned cold and unfamiliar as he ordered my mom to get me exorcised of whatever evil was inside me, leading me astray from the right path. Heartbroken, I bent to my parents' wishes. I married and brought my new husband with me to Minneapolis. Only when I resumed my second year at university did I find the courage for my first act of defiance. Since my dad had insisted on handing me over to another man, he could no longer dictate what I was studying. I switched out of the business track that he'd compelled me to pursue and declared an English major. I enrolled in creative writing classes and, when a professor pulled me aside after class to tell me I had a gift, I allowed myself, for the first time in my life, to envision what I might want for myself. Two years later, when the offer came from the director of the MFA program in the Pacific Northwest for a free ride, I filed for divorce and packed up my belongings, the handwoven rugs from Kashmir, a camel-bone jewelry box from the mountain resort town of Shimla, my collection of books. I knew I wasn't coming back, not to my parents' house in Minneapolis, and not to my parents' house in the Old City. So I took little pieces of home with me.

A decade after my arranged marriage, when my brain was stunned and damaged, the amnesia stripping me of my recent memories and flinging me back to my distant past, during those days when I was screaming "no husband" and when I was throwing tantrums and pushing Scott away, I can't help but wonder if it wasn't really him that I was denying.

# 54

When I was twenty-six and planning my wedding to Scott, I kept thinking back on my arranged marriage. The fireworks, the brass band, the costume changes over the five days—and so the second time around I kept it simple. On the morning of the wedding, Scott and I held a private Nikah ceremony at a small mosque on Alemany Street in San Francisco. Only his parents and my mom attended. I wore a cotton kurta and simple gold hoops. No one could have guessed that I was a bride and that this small gathering was a wedding party. Inside the mosque, the five of us sat cross-legged in a small circle on the soft carpet of the main sanctuary. Covered in a peacock-green cotton headscarf, I sat next to Scott. The Nikah was brief. The imam asked me if I consented to being married and, without any hesitation, I said yes. Instead of a religious Nikah-nama, like the kind my dad had signed for me as my guardian the first time around, the imam signed our California marriage license. And while the Nikah-nama might have required two men as witnesses, our two moms served as the official witnesses to our union.

Later that afternoon, in the back garden of Scott's childhood home in Palo Alto, we celebrated with a public exchange of vows in front of our close friends and family, including my two brothers. For that ceremony, rather than sit on a dais like I did the first time, with my head modestly lowered and covered by a veil of jasmine, I instead strode jubilantly down the aisle, dressed in a silk organza sari, my neck and ears and wrists flashing gold and emeralds, fresh magnolia flowers from his mom's garden in my hair. A tabla and a sitar player we'd hired for the ceremony played a classical Indian raga.

During the outdoor reception that followed, I was so giddy that I couldn't pay attention to Scott's father's toast, a poem he'd written and was reciting in our honor, describing how our love had transcended superficial differences to bring us together, first Scott and me, and then our two families. I couldn't get over how happy I was—such a stark contrast to the unhappiness I'd felt during my arranged marriage. I kept touching Scott, some part of me making sure he was really there. It all felt so unreal. In one of those moments, when I was standing in his arms underneath an ancient and sturdy redwood tree, the two of us smiling at each other, the camera went off. The photographer had caught us. Unlike the wedding photos we'd posed for, this one was so raw with emotion that we ended up framing it.

That photograph was displayed on the tall cherrywood dresser in our master bedroom, where I was holed up upon returning from the hospital, convalescing. It stood right next to the camel-bone jewelry box in which I stored my wedding rings. My gaze kept returning to these items, but I didn't understand why.

## 55

I started to notice other photographs framed around the house, several hanging in the hallway between the bedroom and bathroom, others placed on the fireplace mantel, and one on the rattan table next to the armchair upholstered in indigo shibori fabric. Scott was a talented photographer who took up the hobby to document his adventures when he first began traveling solo as an undergraduate. He had such a natural gift that even without formal training several of his photographs had won prizes and been featured in travel magazines. That he was able to transcend language to convey an emotion, a creative feat I could never achieve, was one of the reasons I was drawn to him. In our five years together, he'd shot hundreds of photos, capturing every rite of passage—our honeymoon in Provence, his mom's memorial service, and, shortly thereafter, his dad's memorial service, our first house, the baby shower.

Now that two weeks had passed since my discharge, the grogginess and headaches were gradually subsiding, leaving me alert for short bursts of time. When I made my tentative way to the bathroom with my mom's help or even, begrudgingly, Scott's help, or when I lounged out in the living room for a change of scenery, I found myself staring at these photographs. An image of us standing at the edge of a cliff near the Anasazi ruins in Chaco Culture National Historical Park in New Mexico. A shot of us with his parents on a hike on Lands End Trail, the Golden Gate Bridge in the background. In another framed photo, I was nine months pregnant and enormous, my body carrying both the baby weight and the edema from the illness that I didn't yet know was ravaging my organs. My face covered in sweat, I was pointing at a sign indicating the elevation of the mountain Scott and I had just climbed, close to 9000 feet. The photo wasn't particularly flattering. Scott framed it only because he thought it remarkable that I'd made my slow way up to the summit with my huge belly. Along the way, almost every hiker we encountered joked that the strain of the hike would induce labor, that I'd end up giving birth right on that mountain. Soon enough, Scott was flashing his Swiss Army knife and gleefully announcing that he was looking forward to cutting the umbilical cord.

Now that I was growing more alert, my procedural memory was kicking in and I was starting to notice that something was off, although I couldn't quite put my finger on exactly what it was. Muscle memory misled me, assuring me I could walk and speak and, over and again, I fell for it, fell over my own feet, fell over my words. Why couldn't I jump out of bed like I used to and stride down the hallway? Why was my mom with me in the bathroom every time I went, holding on to me tightly as I sat hunched over on the toilet, the heavy weight of gravity seeming to push me downward to the floor? Why did she and Scott have to help me change my clothes? When I reached out to grab the cup of warm milk my mom made for me every evening, why was the cup never where I thought it would be?

Those questions led my gaze back to the photos. It didn't register that it was me I was looking at because I wasn't really absorbing the entire image. I was instead taking in pieces of *her*, the person I'd once been, this phantom haunting me from different frames, staring at her legs, her hands, her belly. I was cutting her up and dissecting different parts of her body, as though trying to understand how they worked.

My neurologist had suggested that my memories would return gradually. That was not my experience. A little over two weeks after I'd left the hospital, I was sitting in the living room in the armchair while my mom was cooking chicken curry for dinner. Ishmael was napping in the nursery. In my hands was the framed photograph from my wedding. I had carried it out with me from where it usually sat on the dresser in the bedroom. I was studying it when the front door opened and Scott walked in, arrived home from work. That was all it took. All at once, he existed inside the framed photo in my hands and he had materialized out of nothing to stand before me. I blinked. In the seconds it took for him to greet me and my mom, my brain clicked together stray puzzle pieces and my memories returned so rapidly that it was like watching a movie on hyper speed. There I was, meeting Scott for the first time at the evening reception welcoming new students to the graduate writing program, my attraction to him so immediate and so raw that I found myself making an excuse to rush away from him. There he was, following me and coaxing me into conversation, asking me to meet him the next day for coffee. There we were, meeting for coffee, and soon enough sharing our writing with each other, falling in love through these vulnerable admissions on the page—like that, my brain replayed pivotal moments, covering our five years together so swiftly that, as a neurological reflex, my body went absolutely still while my eyes blinked uncontrollably like a camera shutter, documenting it all—now here we were, winding down the Pacific Coast Highway, having skipped the graduation ceremony, and now there, moving into our first home nestled in the Twin Peaks hills. Along with the memories came the emotions and it was as though I was falling in love all over again, nervous and giddy at the same time, excited for our life together. My body felt lifted with joy until the last memories flashed and suddenly there I was, up in that dreaded penthouse delivery suite, crushed under the pain of my imploding body, one eye closed against the double vision as I tried to a catch a glimpse of my son while he was being weighed and bathed by a nurse.

While my medical records show that I emerged to consciousness on the night of the fifth day of the coma, this moment when my memories returned, abruptly, unceremoniously, is when it felt to me like I had woken up.

# 56

I called out to Scott and rose from the chair and, just as quickly, tricked again by my former self, by memories of what I could once do, I fell flat onto the ground, right on top of the thick Kashmiri rug. I was bereft. I was outraged. Without any means to control my emotions, a deep sorrow welled up inside of me, taking over my being, and I wept like a child. At the same time, another self was inhabiting my body, and she was absolutely rational. This self was watching me, wondering why I was throwing a tantrum. Years after this incident, when I described this bizarre feeling of being divided to my neurologist on a follow-up visit, he theorized that under the strain of the global cerebral trauma the separate islands of neurons in my head were essentially acting as they might in a split brain. A split brain is one in which the corpus callosum connecting the two hemispheres is disconnected or severed to some degree, making it so the right and left brain each have their own reality: individual perceptions, concepts, and impulses to act. Rather than working together, each hemisphere then works independently. Like that, my neurologist believed that separate areas in my brain were functioning separately from one another, tracking different realities, comprehending at different levels. This was why I was both on the ground, mourning everything I'd lost, and also observing myself dispassionately, unaware that I'd lost anything. A broken brain doesn't know it's broken. Overcoming amnesia didn't mean I'd overcome other neurological deficits to perceive my reality.

My crying brought my mom running from the kitchen. It woke Ishmael from his sleep. Scott was instantly at my side. Rather than push him away, I grabbed him and held him like I'd never held him before. Astonished by my response to him, relieved over what it meant, he dropped next to me on the rug and cradled me in his arms. I buried my face in his chest and inhaled deeply, savoring the familiar scent of his skin. Seeing us, my mom whispered a prayer of gratitude and retreated from the room, saying she was going to tend to Ishmael.

*Ishmael?* How was I going to care for my newborn? I started to cry all over again. I continued to watch myself cry from a distance.

"Why are you crying?" Scott asked, perplexed. "I'm so happy right now."

I shook my head, confused. How could I explain that I didn't know what I was grieving.

In the days that followed, I was ever aware of the two minds inside me. When I held my son, I was heartbroken that I couldn't breastfeed him and, simultaneously, conscious that

I felt no bond. When I began trying to nurse him, hoping the milk would come, I couldn't understand why I was having so much trouble with my vision. A black splotch prevented me from making out his face. My lack of depth perception meant I kept mistaking where his mouth was and found myself pushing my breast into his cheek or chin. Now that I recalled who he was, Scott moved back into our bed, but we slept with my maternity pillow between us to prevent him from accidentally bumping my head while tossing and turning in his sleep. I agreed this was a good idea and I also thought it strange that he was concerned about my head. When I was sitting beside my mom on the sofa, I purposely held her hand, not caring if she flinched, needing her to know how grateful I was for her help. At the same time, when a friend stopped by with groceries or homemade dinner, I told them not to make such a fuss: women had been having babies since the dawn of time! My feet weren't working. I couldn't time my movements. My tongue wasn't working. The wrong word would pop out. My short-term memory wasn't working. I told my mom that my milk still hadn't come and she'd have to heat up a bottle of formula. Minutes later, I told my mom that my milk still hadn't come and she'd have to heat up a bottle of formula. My memory wasn't working. I answered the phone and a woman told me her name and asked how I was. I panicked and handed the phone to Scott. *I don't know her. She's confused*, I later told him. *She's a local writer*, he said. *You met her through your agent.* I decided that Scott was as confused as the woman.

Threaded through every moment was this line of double thinking. I was both attempting to pick up pieces of my life to find some way to carry on while simultaneously insulated from the shattering. But my mistakes were adding up. I was stumbling over my feet, stumbling over my words. I was desperate to know why I'd lost control of my body. Two realities of me coexisted inside my head, one who could properly work her limbs and vision and senses and one who couldn't. But there was only one blundering about her house. And that meant there was only one me. The realization, when it came, purged my phantom self from my being, leaving me whole and also wholly broken.

Miracle Girl, that was what they called me at the hospital. Miracle Girl, I thought bitterly, must be medicalese for freak.

## 57

I didn't recognize myself. Whenever I went to the bathroom now, I tried not to look at my reflection, but I couldn't help it. The edema had drained out of my organs and body. My eyes and nose were no longer sunk under my bloated flesh but were now bulging forth from my face. I was emaciated. I'd not only dropped all forty-five pounds of my pregnancy weight but was still losing more weight every day. I was down to ninety-four pounds, the same weight I'd been in middle school. But I didn't have a young girl's robust body. Nor did it show any signs that I'd just delivered a baby. I couldn't nurse my son, my breasts were shriveled and limp. My ribs protruded from my chest. When I circled my waist with my two hands, my fingertips touched. My calves were as thick as my wrists. I was nothing but rattling bones. I was on the Death Diet. My body had been preparing for the grave and hadn't expected that modern technology would keep it alive.

The benefit of a split perception was that it had saved me from sinking into depression. Without that buffer, my emotions morphed raw and unfiltered. I didn't have the maturity of mind to control myself. I mourned as though I was standing over my own grave, witnessing my own burial. I asked my mom to walk around the house and remove all the photographs of me that were displayed. I didn't want to look at them—at *her*—anymore. Once the photos came down, however, I started to understand that removing them didn't matter. Since I lacked the higher mental processes to visualize a future, all I had left was my past. Even in my mind, I was bumping into my old self. There was no doctor or faith healer who could put the various broken pieces of this body back together. They'd all given up on me. And that made me think that I should give up on myself. No matter how hard I tried to explain this to Scott, encouraging him to leave me, I could tell my poor husband wasn't getting it. When he looked at me, he only saw the woman I'd once been, the one he believed I could be again. The woman he married.

"We're going to do this together."

That's what he kept saying to me. And I didn't have the heart to tell him his words only made me feel more alone. This wasn't our journey, it was mine.

"You're not alone," my mom would assure me whenever she found me crying in bed. "After suffering, God brings ease."

God? There was no hidden meaning to what I was enduring, no higher purpose. There is no God, I wanted to enlighten her. No god, anyway, that would let this happen to me.

# 58

In my Catholic high school in suburban Minneapolis, every year on the first day of Lent, I attended mass in the school gymnasium with my classmates. From where I sat in the bleachers, I watched the priest position himself behind a wooden podium set up on the gleaming basketball court. Dressed in purple robes representing penance, he preached about the significance of the Lenten season. Lasting forty days, Lent represents the period of time, he told us, from when Jesus withdrew into the desert up to the days of his crucifixion and death.

"Ash Wednesday is a solemn reminder," the priest sermonized every year, "of our mortality." Mass began in this way on Ash Wednesday with the priest first reading from Joel—"Return to me with your whole heart, with fasting, and weeping, and mourning"—and ended with "Remember you are dust, and to dust you shall return. In the name of the Father, the Son, and the Holy Ghost."

Even as the priest instructed us to reflect on our mortality, we were also, he said, to prepare to celebrate Jesus's resurrection at the feast of Easter. Jesus conquering death symbolized our own resurrection in heaven. This miracle was undeniable proof of Christ's two natures: he was both man born of Virgin Mary and also God from before time began—although, again miraculously, his human body and human soul did not mix with his divinity but were instead combined in hypostatic union. After mass, I walked through the hallways, going from class to class bearing an ash cross on my forehead. I never saw anything wrong with receiving the ashes. Although I didn't believe that Jesus was divine, as a Muslim I shared many Christian beliefs about Jesus: that he was born of the Virgin Mary, that he performed miracles, that he will return on the Day of Judgment to lead believers to the kingdom of God. In Islam, Jesus is honored as a penultimate prophet. I received the ashes because I was taught at home to believe in what they represented: repentance, death, and renewal.

It was my Catholic education that made me realize that it wasn't just Muslims who revered the martyred body. Because early Christians were persecuted by the Romans, any Christian who died at the hands of the Romans was considered a martyr, their blood regarded as sacred because the sacrifice imitated Christ's own death and resurrection. Having died for their beliefs, a martyr was automatically granted the status of saint and guaranteed a spot in heaven—a concept later echoed by Muslims, who also claimed that any person who died for the cause of Islam was a martyr and went straight to paradise. This eternal fate led some Christians, including the Bishop Ignatius of Antioch in the first century CE, to obsessively wish to become martyrs themselves.

Growing up as an outsider in the United States, I picked up on this long-established spiritual narrative of martyrdom and resurrection. As a South Indian girl, I accepted that death was all people ever talked about. As a Midwestern girl, I knew that death was a taboo subject no one talked about—and no one in the U.S., especially not my classmates at Catholic school, admitted to being religious. And yet Jesus's sacrifice seemed to be everywhere: in the TV shows I watched, the art we viewed on field trips to local museums, the best-selling books we read in class. In C. S. Lewis's *The Lion, the Witch and the Wardrobe*, Aslan is killed by the White Witch only to rise up and vanquish his enemy. In *The Lord of the Rings*, the wizard Gandalf dies on Zirakzigil and, just like Aslan, he returns to life even more powerful than before. And, of course, in the book that served as inspiration for my son's name, after Captain Ahab's ship, the *Pequod*, is sunk, Ishmael floats to safety on a coffin he uses as a life raft. He must literally embrace death if he is to have a second chance at life.

Over the years, whenever I've shared the story of my own brush with death, I've found that no one wants to hear those parts that deal with the struggle and heartache and loss that's inherent in bringing about a new life. I've gotten used to being asked to skip over those unglamorous details, to hurry and get to the end where I'm the perfect image of the romanticized body: miraculously resurrected as whole and complete. But it's those dark days that I can't seem to forget even after two decades, when I came so close to giving up on myself.

Often in life when I'd felt sad and alone, I had turned to outside narratives, searching for solace and insights, comfort to endure what I was going through. During my rehabilitation, however, had I tried to shake off the grief by opening a glass door to a bookcase and thumbing through one of our many books, how many words would I have been able to accurately string together and make sense of? Without the higher capacities to think and imagine, those abilities that separate us from animals, how much of the human experience explored in those books would I have been able to identify with, and how much had become foreign to me? Stories were meaningless. Stories had no place in my life.

## 59

Late one Saturday evening, after my mom and Ishmael had turned in for the night, Scott suggested we have a date. He thought it might cheer me up if we spent some time together reconnecting. The word *date* instantly triggered memories of our past—not the different restaurants or concerts we'd gone to, but the emotions of joy and excitement, the lightheartedness of those hours spent together, and I readily agreed.

He popped in a DVD of a film he'd rented at Blockbuster and we sat together on the sofa. For a moment, as I snuggled into him, it did feel like old times and I found myself feeling lighter. But it didn't take long for me to realize that my brain had tricked me once again. Within minutes of the movie starting, I lost the thread of the plotline. And the more I struggled to pick up the narrative thread, the faster my heart raced in panic. I kept this hidden from Scott. He'd lit candles and dimmed the lights. He'd rented a romantic comedy called *Notting Hill*. He was doing his best to make this a special evening. Confessing that this had been a mistake would only crush him, making him again feel like he was alone in our marriage. Having a baby was supposed to bring us together, transforming us into a family. Instead it had torn the family apart, putting up barriers where I'd never imagined barriers could be.

So I lay in his arms and pretended to enjoy the movie. I smiled when I heard him laughing to fool him into believing I was following along. But I was really looking around at our house, taking in what we had built together. Making an accounting of all I had lost. There were the books Scott and I had collected through the years, carefully arranged by genre in the glass-doored bookcases. There was my mother-in-law's artwork on the walls alongside Scott's photographs, both of which had once inspired my own creativity. Now, day after day, my computer sat unused. No words or sentences passed through my head. Thoughts had gone quiet, replaced with strong, often uncontrollable emotions.

Weighing only about three pounds, the average human brain is composed of over 500 trillion neural connections, performing a dizzying array of complex mental processes every zeptosecond. Each neuron is like a tiny tree, whose branches reach out and touch the branches of other neurons, creating between 5,000 and 10,000 connections. Those connections essentially make up who we are: our sensations in the world as well as our perceptions of our world, how we think and how we feel, how we reason and how we emote, how we learn, how easily we can pick up new languages and skills, how long or short a time we can stay focused, our ability to walk and speak, our memory, which is essentially a pattern of connections between neurons—everything is controlled by the brain.

"Cogito, ergo sum," wrote René Descartes. "I think, therefore I am."

To think, I needed to string together ideas. And to have an idea, I needed the capacity to interpret the world around me. And to interpret the world around me, I needed neurons to send and receive electrical impulses through a complicated web of communication. The outermost layer of the cerebrum is the cerebral cortex, the gray matter of the brain. The deep folds and wrinkles increase the surface area of the gray matter, granting us greater power to process greater information. Without my brain assigning meaning to what I was seeing and hearing and experiencing, the elegant composition and form in my mother-in-law's artwork dissolved into splotches of competing colors and textures and shapes. Conversations streaming from the movie no longer engaged and delighted me, but instead mutated into pure noise that brought on a headache. All value and meaning were lost as my world turned flat and myopic and bleak.

Off in the distance, down the hall and in the second bedroom, there was the subtlest of movements, nearly imperceptible, my son stirring awake. Always, his crying started off softly, with not enough force to rouse my mom. But I was alert to his needs. I heard him now over Julia Roberts's flirtations with Hugh Grant on the screen. I heard him when I was sleeping soundly in the back bedroom, his cry startling me awake even when I was in deep sleep. In the darkness, from across the house, I'd lie awake and listen to him whimpering next to my mom, asking to be fed, to be changed. While my mom slept through his fussing, I'd observe myself, detached from my body, to see if I might feel some maternal impulse to go to him. I was relieved when there was nothing. That emptiness was preferable to the hungry rage that possessed my body when I was feeling weak and threatened by his existence.

My mom now woke up. I heard her cooing to him, then the sound of her slippers sliding across the hardwood as she made her way to the kitchen. He fussed the whole while it took to heat up a bottle, as though he hadn't eaten in days. What would he remember of these weeks, what impressions were being imprinted on his developing brain? What was it like for him to encounter the world for the first time, all the chattering and the lights and the colors and the sounds? Was he able to process this chaotic stream of sensory data better than me, his brain blossoming, my brain shriveling? We have a romanticized vision of the beginner's mind. When we see babies, we see a world of possibilities that lay before them. They can grow up to be anything they want to be! But I didn't see possibilities. Only a terrifying nothingness.

# 60

Six weeks after my discharge from the hospital, I had my first follow-up appointment with neurology. Scott took the day off from teaching to take me. It was the first time I'd left the house since coming home and, while Scott drove, I stared out the window at the familiar sights of cafés and corner stores and soon forgot where we were headed. The fluid motion of the car was so recognizable that I even forgot about my physical limitations. It was as though the windshield was a portal and I'd slipped through. For those brief seconds, I was back inside my old body, back to being me. The sun was shining. The air was warm. People were gathered outside restaurants waiting to be seated for brunch. A mother, dressed in Lycra running pants and top, was jogging while pushing her child in a three-wheel jogger stroller. What a great idea, I thought. I'm going to take my son on a run tomorrow. I was so disoriented—traveling on some strange neural highway miles from my current reality—that when Scott pulled into the parking lot of the hospital, I asked him why we'd come. Was he not feeling well?

Before the appointment with neurology, I had a follow-up visit with obstetrics to assess how I was recovering from the delivery. As expected, the obstetrician who delivered my son was nowhere to be seen, even though Scott peeked down various hallways and into doorways, hoping to finally confront him. He and my dad had talked at length about suing the hospital but, in the end, Scott had decided against it. The time and effort and emotions we would expend caught up with attorneys and courtrooms, he concluded, would be better spent on my recovery and on raising our son. The only reason Scott was searching for the OB who delivered Ishmael was because he was hoping for an apology. He just wanted an acknowledgment. We both did. So it irked him that the doctor was still nowhere to be found and, after my exam, when the young obstetrician who examined me was washing her hands and saying that I was recovering nicely from the delivery and everything looked normal, I heard Scott guffaw. For a few long moments, the room went uncomfortably silent.

Finally, the obstetrician said, "I mean, the stitches are healing up nicely."

After that appointment, I underwent another hour-long MRI scan of the brain while Scott graded student essays in the waiting room. This was so the neurologist I was scheduled to see could compare the results to previous ones performed while I'd been a patient in the hospital to determine if there had been any alleviation to the swelling. As it turned out, there hadn't been any alleviation, which meant that, even after six weeks recuperating at home, I was little better off than when I'd been discharged.

The neurologist was now sitting on a stool directly in front of me with my thick medical file on his lap. He was new to my case and had taken several long minutes to review my file while Scott and I sat silently next to each other on two white plastic chairs. When he finished, he drew in a deep breath and patted my arm sympathetically before scooting his stool close to where I was sitting, his knees a wrists' width from my own.

"I'm going to say a list of five words, one after another," he said, looking me intently in the eyes. "After I say a word, I want you to repeat the word. Pay attention and try to remember the word. At the end, I'll ask you to recount as many of the five words as you can. Do you understand?"

"Yes," I replied, focusing my efforts on keeping my face from revealing what I was thinking. I was like a child again; it wasn't as easy to hide my emotions as it had once been. I didn't want to offend the neurologist, who had a kind face and had taken to heart what I'd been through. A damaged brain doesn't have the ability to assess its own damage, so I easily slipped into memories of what I was capable of doing. I couldn't help but think he sounded overly concerned. All I had to do was recall five words. I couldn't imagine how I wouldn't pass this neurological assessment with flying colors.

"I'm going to begin now," the neurologist said. "Remember, say the word after me. Clock," he slowly enunciated.

"Clock," I repeated as he'd asked.

"Kiwi," he said, after a second's pause.

"Kiwi," I again repeated slowly, making sure the word came out correctly.

Once again, he paused half a beat, giving me the chance to absorb the word before he went on. "Rock," he finally said.

"Rock," I said after him.

Over the years of my recovery, I've learned that there are many theories regarding the different types of memories we have in our brain. The briefest is sensory memory, which might hold a sensation—the sound of footsteps on the sidewalk or the sight of a bird on a branch—for no more than a second. If we don't pay attention, the sound we hear or the sight we glimpse vanishes from the mind. Think about it: Can you recall what specific sounds you heard in the last sixty seconds? Thirty seconds? It's only when we pay attention that the world we move through gets more fully processed and becomes stored as short-term memory. Information we store in short-term memory can last for several hours to several days—the reason short-term memory is so effective when we're cramming for an exam. The neurologist was being deliberate with his enunciation and timing to help me to fully absorb each word I'd just repeated. He wanted my full attention on what I was saying to help the words move past sensory memory. In this way, he was testing if I'd recovered from my short-term memory loss.

After he'd said the fifth and final word, he removed a slender penlight from his white coat pocket. He shone it directly into my eyes to examine my pupils, then asked me to follow the light from right to left, left to right, and up and down.

"Okay," he said, slipping the penlight back into his pocket. "Now that it's been several seconds, take your time and see if you can recall what words I listed. Tell me as many as you are able. Can you do that?"

I smiled. "Of course," I said, glancing at Scott. He squeezed my hand in encouragement.

"Great! Let's hear them," the neurologist said.

It's in long-term memory that we store our sense of ourselves, made up of autobiographical information, such as events from our childhood and beyond, our school studies, our general knowledge of the world, even personal facts—like the facts that I'd been born in the Old City and was writing a book and married to Scott and had a son. The memories we store, however, are hardly continuous. We usually remember what we remember because of strong emotions we'd experienced at the time. The hormones that are released when you feel strong emotions intensify the memories attached to them. This explains why, during an era when the connections in my brain were faulty and my short- and long-term memory were not functioning properly, I am still able to remember certain incidents from the early weeks and months of my recovery. And one of those things that I clearly remember is how I couldn't remember a single word from the five the neurologist had listed.

The doctor saw this on my face. "Take your time," he said, patiently. "There's no rush."

Scott squeezed my hand again. "You can do this," he reassured me. "You just said the words."

But that was the trouble. There was no "just" for me. No tip-of-the-tongue sensation. No vague recollection of what I might have heard. No words chomping at the bit like when I was writing my novel. Pick me! Pick me! No alternative choices: Might he have said this? Was it this? No clues: it rhymes with this, is related to this. There was only a void. A room so dark you can't see your hand in front of your face. Even as I was still participating in the exam, the exam was disappearing. Rather than stacking up, the present moment was collapsing and slipping away. I went from feeling cavalier that I'd pass with flying colors to utterly alarmed. What would happen if I couldn't catch up to the present moment?

"What's a fruit you don't particularly like?" Scott asked as a way of helping me.

I stared at him.

"Let's move on with the exam," the neurologist suggested. From the same pocket as the penlight, he now pulled a reflex hammer and began checking my reflexes. From there, he evaluated several cranial nerves. He asked me to stick out my tongue and speak, then placed his hands next to my face like horse blinders and asked me to turn my head left and right against the resistance. While I couldn't tell how well I was performing with these particular assessments, it was clear even to me that I failed in my motor functions. I lacked balance and coordination, so I had to hold on to the exam table to shuffle forward in the straightest line I could manage, which was embarrassingly clumsy. It was how I'd been stumbling about the house this past week, by holding on to furniture and using the walls for support. After several long minutes, we were back in our seats and the neurologist ended the exam by asking me to reach out and touch his finger with my own. He held his index finger about half a foot in front of my face . . . or so it seemed. Without the proper functioning of my peripheral vision, I couldn't quite locate his finger. I kept stabbing at the air, fruitlessly.

Finally, the neurologist rolled his stool back to his desk and began jotting down the results of the exam into my medical file. I turned and looked at Scott. He shifted nervously in his chair then, as though in afterthought, flashed me a weak smile.

"You did great," he said. "Better than you ever did while in the hospital."

I didn't have a memory of having taken these neurological exams in the hospital. The only memories I had to compare my performance to were of who I'd been before. Pre-Samina. Pre-Delivery. That Samina had followed me into this exam room like a ghost. That Samina had smirked when she'd been given the task to remember five words. Five words? What were five insignificant words? I'd memorized whole poems and sonnets and paragraphs of literature. I'd memorized lengthy, meandering chapters of the Qur'an in Arabic. I'd memorized long lists of Hindi songs from popular Bollywood movies. In high school, I'd been at the top of my French class. And yet it was those very five words—words so common that I'd used them countless times in my everyday life, words so remarkable that they'd effectively vanished from memory—that now made me feel like I was clinging to the edge of my humanity.

The neurologist closed the medical file and ran his palms up and down the front of the folder. He was waiting patiently to see if I had any questions. After the various neurological assessments, the exam room felt quiet and still. Outside the closed door, along the corridor, I heard footsteps followed by a woman's laughter. Scott caressed my back.

I swallowed and focused my mind on what I wanted to say. I listened to myself rehearsing the words in my head before I said them aloud. "When will I," I asked haltingly, hoping my aphasia wouldn't make me trip over any words, "write again?"

Scott let out a loud snort of surprise. He was completely taken aback by the question. On his face, I could see what he was thinking. There is so much else to worry about!

My neurologist rolled his stool closer and sat facing me, eye to eye again. "The MRI scan doesn't show any improvements," he said, watching me closely to see if I was registering what he was saying. "There is still evidence of cerebellar fluid collection. Visually, you're presenting with bilateral hand tremor and ptosis of the right eye. The neurological assessment, while showing improvement from previous ones," he said, nodding at Scott, "is still far from where it needs to be—"

"Write again?" I pressed, interrupting him.

"When a person suffers a stroke, about two million nerve cells die in the brain. An average stroke involves about three cubic inches of tissue. I'm afraid the damage you've suffered is not contained to a single area. The damage is diffuse—think of it like a traumatic brain injury. The global injury you've suffered is similar to that, as though you've been in a terrible car accident. With the current levels of edema, I would venture to say that it will take up to a year, if not more, for your brain to get back down to normal size. Only at that point will we have a better idea of what functions you've permanently lost."

"Or not lost," Scott said, jumping in. "She could recover fully."

The neurologist glanced at Scott then back at me. "Every patient is different," he said carefully. "Two people with the exact same head injury will recover differently. Recovery is based on a variety of tangible factors, like age and underlying health, but also on intangible factors, like a patient's will and determination. In the end," he added, "a patient has to want to recover. You have a son, right?"

I nodded.

"In your son," he said, "you have an inherent reason to want to recover. These first six months following injury are crucial. This is when the brain makes remarkable leaps in recovery. So, take advantage of the remaining four months of this window."

The more the neurologist talked, the more I found myself losing the thread of the conversation. I peered into his face, trying to piece his words together with their meaning. But I found myself fatigued. This was the most activity I'd had since I'd woken up in the neuro-ICU. I was slumping in my chair. The ptosis he'd pointed out was getting worse and I could feel my eyelid drooping even lower over my right eye, obstructing my vision. A headache was coming on. I wanted nothing more than to stretch out on the exam table and close my eyes.

"Writing?" I asked, pushing out the word with the little strength I had. Disconnected puzzle pieces. Broken neural pathways. Along with my brain, my life had become an island of its own. No one knew what it felt like to be looking out at the world from inside my head. The same world from a different head. As kind and patient as he was, the neurologist had only studied brain trauma. He'd only ever experienced it from the outside. His assessments merely evaluated my nervous system, fell short from making a thorough evaluation of what my body could no longer do. How able was I, for instance, to resume being a wife when it wasn't possible to be intimate with my husband? And if Scott could look past my disabilities, was it even possible to seduce the man who'd become my caregiver? Without the capacity to care for myself, I had regressed into a childlike state. It was the only comfort I had right now, to pout, to cry, to complain, to have my mom hold me and rock me and to smell her skin and to hear her pray for me when I couldn't get myself to pray. She fell naturally into the role of my nurturer. I fell naturally into being cared for. But how would that old role now guide me in becoming a mother to my own son?

The neurologist sighed, his chest rising and falling slowly. "To write," he said after a moment's consideration, "you need this part of your brain and this part and this part and this part." He was pointing to various areas of his head. "As I said, the damage is diffuse." He put up a hand to stop

Scott from interrupting him. "Even after other functions return—motor functions seem to return more quickly, for instance—but even after those functions return, from the scale of the damage, I'm not optimistic you'll get your higher faculties back. Those faculties you need to process thought, to imagine, to visualize a future, to create, to reason and use logic, the very tools you need in order to write."

His words should have devastated me. But instead I found myself thinking, what does he know? How many exam rooms like this one had I sat in during the past year, alone or with Scott? First being assured that I was fine. Now being assured I was not fine. Why would I continue to trust these doctors? Too upset to look at the neurologist, I stared down at my hands. My blackened nails were growing out and exposing the healthy pink nails that were coming in. Back when I was seven months pregnant, the first symptom I noticed of eclampsia was the swelling of my hands. I'd been typing away on my novel, my arms stretched past my big belly, when I began noticing a strange discomfort. That had been the last day I'd worked on my book.

*Pilgrimage*

# 61

In 1587, a eunuch named Yakut in the court of the Qutub Shahi dynasty fell ill. The Qutub Shahi court at that time was located inside the Golconda fortress, about eleven kilometers from where my dad's house now stands in the Old City. Yakut was well-loved at court and a great many remedies were tried to cure him, both with traditional ayurvedic doctors as well as spiritual healers. But his health continued to deteriorate. The king and the courtesans grew alarmed. Soon enough the situation became so hopeless that there was nothing left to do but pray.

On the very night when it looked like all was lost, Yakut, in a state of delirium, had a dream. A saintly man in green robes appeared and asked Yakut to visit him at the summit of a nearby mountain. It was a dome-shaped mountain made of slate-gray granite, barren of vegetation. In the dream, Yakut scaled the approximately two thousand feet, where the saintly man was sitting waiting for him at the summit, his hand resting on a stone. The man revealed himself to Yakut as Hazrat Ali, the Prophet's son-in-law. The reason he was here, he told Yakut, was in answer to everyone's prayers. The following morning, Yakut told the king about his dream. The king immediately ordered that Yakut be taken to the mountain. At the summit, where Yakut had seen the vision of Ali in his dream, sitting with his hand on a stone, was now an imprint of a hand carved into a stone. Yakut fell to his knees. By morning, he was cured.

Word spread like wildfire. The mountain became sacred. Soon, hundreds of pilgrims of all faiths and backgrounds were trekking to the mountaintop, seeking their own private miracles. Close to five hundred steps were carved into the granite slope taking devotees to the top. A Sufi shrine was constructed around the stone handprint, housing it. The inside of the shrine was decorated with tiles and chandeliers and thousands of little mirrors. The Qutub Shahi kings inaugurated an annual pilgrimage to the site. Nearly three hundred years later, the new rulers of Hyderabad, the Nizams, maintained the tradition of the annual pilgrimage. From their palace in the now-established city of Hyderabad, the Nizams rode to the mountain on top of heavily bejeweled and decorated elephants, followed by a procession of hundreds. The mountain was named Moula ka Pahaar, "Our Lord's Mountain."

This is the sacred mountain where my dad sent imams scurrying up to pray for me by reciting the entire Qur'an.

I have memories of climbing the mountain myself. Moula ka Pahaar is located about sixteen kilometers from my dad's house in the Old City. There was never a visit we made to India without making a pilgrimage to the mountain. My brothers and I would scramble up the 484 steps, zigzagging around other devotees, Hindus and Muslim alike, far outpacing our parents. At the summit, we would stop and catch our breath, stepping off the stairs and onto the smooth granite rock face, warm under the sun. We would stare out at the view of the city while waiting for our parents to arrive. An ancient gateway welcomed visitors into the shrine. Mystics sat cross-legged inside the gateway, in the shade along its wall, praying. In their laps were garlands of white jasmine and candles. My parents would give each of my two brothers and me twenty-rupee notes to hand to the mystics in exchange for a garland and a tea candle.

Stringing jasmine into my hair, I would stand behind my mom in a line with other women, waiting to enter the shrine, while my brothers and my dad stood in a separate line with the men. One by one, we were allowed to go in. When it was my turn, I'd step inside and walk barefoot through the sunlight streaming in from the high windows, cast into shapes of diamonds and scattered across the tiled floor. I'd light my candle at the altar. On the far wall, roped off, a rectangular stone with the handprint was encased behind glass. I would catch only a glimpse of it before being ushered out and into the mosque next to the shrine. In the mosque's small sanctuary, I would stand next to my mom and pray. When we were done, she would nudge me, reminding me to make my wish count. This was a mystical place. Wishes were granted here. Illnesses healed. Barren women made to conceive. When I touched my forehead to the ground, I never doubted in God's mercy—*al rahman, al rahim.*

Now that I'd been stripped of the notion of a merciful God, I was trying, in the days following my neurology visit, to figure out how to reapproach my writing. I'd always believed that writing was sacred. The pen and the book were signs, ayah, miracles. There was even a chapter in the Qur'an entitled "al-Qalam." *Qalam* was the one word I knew that had the same meaning and pronunciation in both Urdu and Arabic: pen. In the first lines of the chapter, God doesn't merely assure the Prophet that he is not insane for having faith, God makes a vow. While we might vow by placing a hand on the Bible or Qur'an, God's vow is "On the pen and what everyone writes" (68:1). I didn't need to climb a mountain to encounter the mystical. I entered that space whenever I wrote. How I now wished to be like Scott and stop believing altogether. In my mind, denying God's compassion was worse than not having any convictions at all because my denial was full of meaning: a sad testament to everything I'd lost.

# 62

There was nothing to do but skip the rituals that usually began my writing day. No meditation. No prayer. No mystical space. No me and God. Just me and my book. Exactly one week after I met with the neurologist, I sat at my desk and listened with delight to the familiar sound of my computer turning on. Muscle memory kicked in. Without realizing, I simply did what I always did when I began my writing day. From years of habit, I automatically scrolled down to the last scene I'd been working on so that I could pick up the narrative thread and stitch it through the following passages, mistakenly believing that I'd easily seep back into the world of my book. How many times would my own brain fool me? There was no need to worry about skipping rituals. I struggled to read the scene while pretending I wasn't struggling. When I was done, I skimmed it a second time, patching together what I missed in my first reading. Then I read it once more. Finally, I stopped and stared at the screen. Did I write this? The novel was based on my arranged marriage and this scene took place on my honeymoon in Madras. That the story was based on my own life experience made no difference. I had no memory of writing it.

Thinking I might have forgotten that particular chapter, I scrolled up through the document and labored through other pages, then scrolled up some more and labored through more pages. Nothing. No recognition that this was my book. It was as though I'd taken a random novel off the bookshelf and begun reading. The scenes I'd written were entirely foreign to me. I felt myself starting to panic and quickly closed the file.

For a long while, I remained sitting at my desk, my hands trembling on the keyboard. I tried not to look at my darkened fingernails. Something meaty and defined was moving through the shadows of my mind. An insight or a decision, I couldn't tell. My neural synapses were firing so slowly that a thought that might have once been instantaneous now took days to be transmitted. I had no choice but to wait and see what it was I was thinking.

# 63

After I moved to San Francisco with Scott and began taking meditation classes at the local Buddhist center to help purge the MFA director's cruel words, it wasn't long before I found myself registering for other classes, these on the teachings of Buddhist philosophy. I wasn't trying to replace Islam. My faith had always been such a big part of my life that it brought with it a set of rituals: the long journeys back to Hyderabad, the pilgrimage to Moula ka Pahaar, the visits to faith healers, Friday prayers at our mosque, Sunday classes at the Minneapolis Islamic Center, a long month of fasting during Ramadan. When I was growing up, my mom often teased my dad, saying, "*Mullah ka dhor masjid tak*," meaning: an imam's only destination is the mosque. We were like that, everything we did revolved around our faith. When I moved out of my parents' house and also stopped returning to India, I hadn't realized how much I missed these old rituals until I sat in my first meditation class at the center and found myself once more immersed in practices and community. Since

Buddhism's roots are in India, it felt like a natural way to fill the gap left in my life, to provide the structure and meaning I craved.

The last class I took at the center was just weeks before I became pregnant. It was an intense session. Students were crying. The entire world seemed to be in mourning. Al-Qaeda operatives had simultaneously denotated two trucks loaded down with more than one thousand pounds of explosives at the U.S. embassies in Nairobi and Dar es Salaam. In addition to approximately one hundred U.S. government workers, hundreds more neighbors and pedestrians had been killed. In response, President Clinton ordered airstrikes against sites linked to Osama bin Laden in Sudan and Afghanistan. None of it made sense. Why had the bodies of innocent men and women and children exploded while they were going about their days? How could their lives have vanished just like that, without any warning? Now bombs were falling from the sky, taking more lives. It was all people could talk about, on the news, with one another. Round and round the conversations went as a way to process the grief.

It was in class that week that I was introduced to the Tibetan concept of bardo, the transitional state between death and rebirth. After death, the consciousness is no longer connected to the physical body. In Tibetan, the word for body is *lu* and means *what's left behind*. After our consciousness leaves behind the body, it continues to subsist in the in-between state of bardo, floating about, darting at great speed, even catching glimpses of the next incarnation. Although I couldn't have known it back when I was taking the class, I was on a direct path to this transitional state, to leaving my body and becoming nothing more than a point of consciousness floating about in an expansive darkness. Depending on the negative karma you've accumulated in your last life, after forty-nine days, you are reborn as a human or an animal or a hungry ghost.

But bardo doesn't merely refer to the physical end of life, our instructor explained that day, trying to help us understand both our immediate reactions to the embassy tragedies as well as a larger, recurring pattern in our lives. Bardo refers to those transitional stages even within our lifetimes. Anytime we feel the rug being pulled out from under us, that feeling of ungroundedness is bardo. Losing a job, losing a baby, losing our money, a marriage coming to an end, a diagnosis of an illness—the very nature of being alive meant we were experiencing successive births and successive deaths. No one is immune. From the moment we are born, every one of us is in a perpetual dance with death—and rebirth. We don't just get one shot at a second chance at life; we get multiple opportunities to do things over and over again, to remake ourselves into what we hope to be.

During class, when students were asked to reflect quietly on the moments of bardo we'd experienced, I made a long list: when my family first immigrated from our home in Hyderabad to Minneapolis, when my dad signed my Nikah-nama marrying me off, when I left my childhood homes to start over in the Pacific Northwest, when I divorced my first husband, when my dad forsook me for marrying Scott. If I'd enrolled in that class just one year later, I would have added:

when I got pregnant and knew right away that something wasn't right, when my life flashed before my eyes on the elevator ride up to labor and delivery on the fifteenth floor, and, lastly, when I woke up—not when I emerged from the coma in the neuro-ICU, but when I overcame my amnesia. On each occasion, I experienced a kind of death.

The fright I'd received in not recognizing my own novel kept me from turning on my computer for several days. Because I was unable to mask my emotions, I'm certain Scott and my mom must have seen the panic on my face. I'm certain they must have fussed over me. But I have no memory of this. No memory of whether or not I continued trying to mother Ishmael, still hoping to nurse him, still hoping to create a bond. What I remember is that my brain conflated events to help me understand what I was feeling. Just like that, without any warning, my novel had exploded and vanished.

# 64

I was back at the computer. In the four days since I'd last sat at the desk, the decision I sensed being made in some remote area of my brain slowly revealed itself. It was simple. Do what I'd done when I couldn't get the MFA director out of my head. Trash the file and start my novel over again.

Onto a fresh document, I typed words and sentences. Since the novel was based on my own experience, I didn't think I needed to use my imagination. Everything I needed was in the past, in the recesses of my brain that I could still access, in my memories. It seemed entirely possible to do this. It felt good to be doing this. Writing a story freed me from my limitations. For the first time, I was outside my broken head, experiencing a different time. Experiencing a different body.

I wrote until I felt hazy with exhaustion, my head pounding so severely I had trouble keeping my eyes open. Although I couldn't have known it at the time, by forcing my brain to put words together, I was also forcing it to create new neural connections. It wasn't an easy process. On that first day, it seemed to me that I'd written for hours on end when in reality I hit my limit in under ten minutes. All physical strength had left me. When I could no longer keep my eyes open from the agony, I swiveled around and let my body slump forward, off the chair and onto the floor. I lay curled up, my arms wrapped around my head, my eyes squeezed tight. In the distance, in some other part of the house, my mom was cooing to my son as she bathed him in the kitchen sink. He was letting out tiny shrieks of joy. I fell asleep to their voices. I awoke half an hour later and found that the pain had lost some of its edge. I crawled to the bed. To lift myself up, I grabbed ahold of the sheets and pulled with all my might.

The next morning and the morning after and the morning after, I did it again. The brief bursts of creativity left me both depleted and inspired. In the late afternoons, after I napped, I sat with my mom on the sofa and watched Bollywood films. Since spoken Urdu and Hindi are nearly indistinguishable, I thought it might be easier to relearn how to follow a narrative thread in my native tongue. At night, when we were in bed together, I'd ask Scott to read me his poems like he used to and, like I used to, I tried to imagine the experience he was recounting, to name the emotion elicited by the verse. The time he stood with Berliners cheering the fall of the Berlin Wall. Hiring a sherpa in Nepal and climbing to Mount Everest Base Camp. Being introduced to me at a reception thrown by the director welcoming incoming students and, from that evening on, finding excuses to bump into me on campus so he could ask me out again. When he detailed these moments now, I couldn't always follow along, but it didn't matter. It was the old routine of reading our work aloud that I relished, of getting so caught up in our writing that we forgot where we were. Some days when Scott was at work, I spread a blanket across the red bricks in the garden and lay in the sun with Ishmael, reading stories to him in English from his baby books. As I did, I challenged myself to say each word correctly. *Hold each letter in your mouth and ear*, I could hear my ayah guiding me. And that's exactly what I did.

# 65

At the neurology exam, the doctor had advised me to take advantage of this six-month window after injury when the brain experiences a heightened state of neural plasticity. While some part of my brain had registered the importance of this time frame, a larger part of me couldn't understand the concept of a clock ticking down.

Did time drag? Or did time fly by? It used to be that I tracked the passage of time in three different languages, Urdu, English, and Arabic, the latter of which, for me, is the language of prayer. In Hyderabad, every morning at dawn, the first *azan* of the day would ring out from the neighborhood mosque, rousing me from bed. After that, each hour the muezzin made the call to prayer, I knew where the sun had moved in the sky. I used to measure and judge time by what I'd achieved, frustrated when I felt my time was wasted or satisfied that time was well spent. There were days during my college years when I had so much on my plate that I was plagued by time—racing against the clock, wanting to turn back the clock—and had to remind myself to stop and breathe. Live in the present moment. And during instances of heightened emotions, like when Scott and I were exchanging wedding vows in the back garden of his parents' home in Palo Alto on a warm summer afternoon, time stood still. When time truly stands still, as it had those first two weeks at home I'd spent convalescing, sleeping day and night like my newborn, it takes on a physical weight, a heft. It's oppressive. Inertia sets in. Without a sense of movement, of progression and purpose, life loses all meaning.

When I could still write, every morning before I sat down to work on my novel, I would light a candle and say a quick prayer. Then I'd center myself with yoga and meditation. I thought these rituals would help my concentration and increase my creativity. More often than not, I'd merely get down on myself for being a bad meditator. I could never fully stop my brain from its internal chatter. My mind would wander off, creating a shopping list or picking out an outfit for that evening's dinner date, never fully in the moment. Now that my body was buzzing with an urgency to recover but my mind was stalled, I wondered if our brains are better off not perceiving a halt in the flow of time. Maybe there's a reason the present moment is so elusive. We naturally project our lives far into the future, even if subconsciously: imagining, dreaming, planning. Ten years from now . . . I will be driving my son to school and will be fully functional again. Five years from now . . . all of this will seem like nothing more than a bad dream. Six months from now . . . my brain will have used this vital window of recovery to regain as many functions as possible. I will be singing lullabies to my son without losing my words to aphasia. I will be carrying him in a front pack as I climb to the summit of Twin Peaks.

Because I couldn't conceptualize a future where I would be whole again, I couldn't use that potential future to inspire me forward. I couldn't run toward my future self. When I now wrote, describing my childhood in the Old City, detailing the five days of my Indian wedding, coaxing memories to emerge onto the page, I was hoping to pave a path forward by rewinding the clock.

# 66

A month after my follow-up with the neurologist, I started to sense that something was off with my book. Maybe I'd been too anthropologic in my description of the five wedding days. Maybe I'd exotified the Old City rituals and beliefs. Maybe my narrator was coming off as unsympathetic. I couldn't pinpoint exactly what was troubling me. Usually, forward momentum helped to bring a concern to light, so I kept going. The more I wrote, however, the more unsettled I became until I had no choice but to stop and read over my work, identify and fix what I'd gotten wrong. It was in examining the manuscript that I saw what it was that was troubling me, an issue so enormous I wondered how I'd missed it before. I paused, considering how to proceed. Then I wrote on with more urgency. My fingers typed away at the keyboard. When I couldn't push myself any longer, I let myself fall off the chair and lay groaning on the ground, curled into myself from the pain in my head. The next morning, I was back at it. My fingers flying on the keyboard. Then my body lying inert on the ground. I was unrelenting. I began ignoring my son in the next room. I batted Scott away when he started reading one of his poems. I only spoke to my mom when I needed something. Even as I refused to give up my old life, I was shutting everyone out. I refused to stop and accept what I could no longer ignore.

The neurologist was right. I couldn't write. The aphasia didn't just scramble words when I spoke. I couldn't type the words I was thinking either. Other words would appear on the screen that weren't even on my mind. Random, unintended words: ice skates instead of Old City, peaches instead of rain. And it got worse: there were times when my brain was too impaired to grasp that the words I was stringing together, sentences that I could see right in front of me on the computer screen, were nothing more than pure nonsense. On occasion, the words weren't even actual words. Just letters smashed together. When I was in the midst of writing, carried away by the prose and the memories, the gibberish actually made sense! Instead of the incoherent sentences and letters, my debilitated brain was convinced it had created some larger meaning. So I'd leave the computer believing that I'd had a breakthrough, that I'd managed to write something worthwhile.

I didn't let myself cry. Crying would prove the doctors right. I confused being stoic with being strong, thinking weakness would only lead me to throwing in the towel, like the doctors had. I was scared. If I couldn't rely on my brain, what did I have left to rely upon? How could I rebuild my life?

Without an answer, I forged ahead recklessly for another

week, chased by a gathering darkness of emotion that I knew would consume me. On and on I went, day after day, word after word, letter after letter, holding them in my mouth and ear, until one morning, I awoke with an all too familiar weight on my chest, securing me to the bed, making it impossible to breathe. I was unable to get myself to the desk and do whatever it was I'd been doing, whatever it was that was clearly not writing. What was the point? When I was still relearning basic tasks like brushing my teeth on my own, using the toilet, walking to the front door, how had I convinced myself that I could write a novel?

I was a writer without words. No words to describe the strange new world I found myself in and no words to reinvent my old one. Even as my brain was stuck in the past, fooling me into believing I was my old self, I would never be my old self again.

# 67

I first began writing stories to help make sense of my life.
When I was a girl and my parents dragged me back and forth
from Minneapolis to Hyderabad, they'd pull me out of one
school and drop me into another every seven or eight months.
In Hyderabad, I was taught Indian history and learned to
write script from right to left, in Urdu. In Minneapolis, I was
taught American history and learned to write script from
left to right, in English. Every time I showed up at school in
Hyderabad after a long absence, a mocking murmur would
ripple through my class: *The American girl is back*. Every time
I showed up at school in Minneapolis, my peers would scoff,
*The Indian girl is back*. I never stayed long enough in either
school to make friends. My parents were oblivious to the
disruption they were causing to my life. I was split down the
middle and, desperate to voice what I was going through, I
started to write stories as a way to stitch myself back together. Depending on where I was in the moment, I wrote the
script from left to right or from right to left. And, sometimes,

I combined both languages. Urdu and English sentences in the same paragraphs, and even in the same lines, crashing into each other, repeating each other, the erratic movement back and forth down the page a visual representation of how I felt.

It never occurred to me that my parents would disapprove. I was twelve when my mom caught me in my room filling up the long summer hours writing stories. She wanted me to go out and play and I told her that I didn't really have any friends. When I went back to my notebook, she didn't ask me to put it away. She instead went to my dad. That was how I knew how serious an offense my writing actually was. My dad sat me down and reminded me of the sacrifices he and my mom had made to immigrate to the U.S.—and they'd suffered, he told me, in order to give us children better lives.

"Don't waste what I've given you by becoming an author," he warned me. As a Muslim, my dad held the art of writing in high regard. As an Indian immigrant, he wanted me to pursue a more practical field, something with the potential to earn a good living, like business.

After that conversation, I began writing in secret. I would lie on the floor in my bedroom, my door closed, hidden from view by my bed. If I heard my mom approaching, I'd stuff the notebook between my mattresses and jump into my desk chair, pretend to be doing my homework. When I left the house, I started hiding my notebooks in the back of my closet, behind my ice skates, or beneath my *shalwars* in the drawer, anywhere I didn't think my mom would look. During my senior year of high school in Minneapolis, at the parent-teacher conference, my English teacher mentioned that she most enjoyed my stories out of the class. *They show such a creative mind!* That was all it took. When I started at university that fall, my dad agreed to pay tuition only if I pursued a business major. Soon after, they arranged my marriage.

So it was with some disbelief that I listened to my mom when she followed me into the bedroom one afternoon and ordered me to sit back down at my desk and continue working on my novel. Almost a week had passed since I'd turned on the computer, since the realization that nothing I wrote made sense. Beholding the disjointed mess was like beholding my scrambled brain. The shock silenced everything inside me, even my strong emotions. As I went about the day, watching Bollywood movies, reading aloud to Ishmael, catching up with my dad and my brothers and Naomi on the phone, cuddling up against Scott in bed, I felt nothing inside. I was just performing as I tried to come to terms with what this meant for my life. Ishmael was entering his fourth month. If the first six months since the trauma were when I could most successfully make advancements, based on the gibberish I was producing, there was no hope that I'd get back my higher mental processes to imagine, to plan, to create, to reason, to think, those very functions that infuse our lives with purpose and meaning.

My mom was now telling me that she could see right through my phony cheer and the fake smiles I'd been flashing these past few days. She teased that I was a worse actress than some of her Bollywood stars. She wouldn't stand for me moping about any longer, not after the joy she'd witnessed in me over the previous weeks when I was working.

Preferring not to worry my mom, I told her that she and my dad had been right all along: writing was a waste of my time. "I've decided to give it up," I announced.

My mom snorted in disbelief. "*Kub chor-na*," she said, dismissing the possibility. She left the room, and thinking that was the end to our conversation, I started to climb into bed, where I'd been spending a good deal of time again. But then she was back carrying Ishmael.

"Tell him you've given up," she said, dropping my son into my arms. Before I could process what was happening, she turned and left again, this time for good.

Now that he'd completed his third month, my son was a hearty sixteen pounds. I had to lean against the bed for support just to bear his weight. He was wiggling about in my arms. I was having trouble holding him right. He was uncomfortable. I kept adjusting my grip, hoping he'd settle down. He was cooing, turning his head this way and that to the slightest sound, the ice maker dropping ice, the wind rustling the broad leaves of the magnolia tree, my mom's voice chatting away on the phone with my dad. The muscles in his neck were strong enough to hold up his head. Fearing I might drop him, I was angling his body across my chest to lay him down when he turned and stared right up at my face. His gaze was so intense that I instantly went still. In his gray-blue eyes, I caught a reflection of myself. I was nothing more than a dark shadow. No distinguishing features. No distinct lines. Just a gloomy shape. It was as though I had finally caught a glimpse of the future. If I continued down this path, putting faith in my deceptive and unreliable brain, where would I end up? Was this shadow how my son would always perceive me? As he grew and developed over the years, learning to walk and learning to speak and learning to play, his brain forging memories of his experiences, his joys and his sorrows, his loves and his heartbreaks, chasing dreams, enduring losses, was I willing to settle for being nothing more than an indistinct presence in the expansive journey of his life, lurking, observing from afar, nothing more than a ghost?

*Fana*

# 68

My body was accustomed to repetition. The first words my dad whispered into my right ear after I was born—*there is no god but God*—were the very words I repeated when I stepped barefoot onto the prayer rug. *"Ashhadan la Ilaha illa'lah . . ."* The meditative, yogic motions of the body—standing, crouching, bowing, standing crouching bowing—marking the sun's movement across the sky from the minute it rose to the very minute it set. When I wasn't praying, I was criss-crossing those very skies, propelled by jet streams from Minneapolis to Hyderabad, from Hyderabad to Minneapolis. My pen's script imitated my motions across the page from right to left, from left to right. Urdu and English and Arabic. The Qur'an itself is a circular narrative with no clear forward momentum, which circles back 600 years to retell the "tales of the ancients."

Repetition is what creates neural connections. Repetition of words. Repetition of movements. Repetition was how to put these puzzle pieces back together. I began by setting modest, unglamorous goals. From the bed, walk the ten paces to the desk. Use as little of the furniture for support as possible. Hold my attention in my physical body. Don't fall into the desk chair with gravity's help. Instead, activate my muscles and my coordination to sit as gracefully as possible. Write for every second I could before the headache rose like a vicious sandstorm and hurled me onto the ground. Afterward, don't crawl to the bed. Rise and walk those ten paces.

The disconnection in various regions of my brain led to a disconnection in my body. Every part seemed to have an intelligence of its own, my hands and feet, my eyes and legs. There was nothing familiar or safe about being in my body and yet here I was, trapped in this foreign body. For days on end, and then for weeks and then eventually for months on end, walk, write, repeat. Walk. Write. Repeat.

I was at once bored by the tedious nature of the tasks. I was at once overwhelmed by the enormous challenge of the tasks, my muscles twitching with exhaustion, sweat moistening my brow. On good days, I wrote for about ten minutes before a headache assaulted me. On bad days, I hit my limit in under five. Time stretched out before me like never before. One day bled into the next, indistinguishable. Simultaneously, time was slipping away. Not only was the six-month window closing in on me, but, as it happened, that six-month mark would land on my thirtieth birthday. Neuroplasticity decreases with age. As a newborn, my son had a brain that was rapidly changing and creating pathways, but by the age of thirty, by my age, that natural plasticity starts to decrease. In more ways than one, I was running out of the very time I found impossible to track.

"The distinction between past, present, and future is only a stubbornly persistent illusion," Albert Einstein said, meaning that time is an undivided reality. How many days did I walk from the bed to the desk, the desk to the bed, before I felt steady on my feet? How many weeks did I sit at the computer and type away, telling myself that it didn't matter, none of it, not the reality that the sentences weren't making any sense, and not that I would have to come back the next day and do it all over again? There were days when I felt more alert than ever, my electrons firing, my feet moving fluidly, almost on their own, almost like before. Days when I would sit and write and feel myself drawn into the imaginary world I was creating. Days when I lounged in the living room or under the warmth of the sun in the back garden, laughing with my mom and my son, with Scott, my life blissfully normal for brief, fleeting minutes.

But there were those days when I'd wake up and everything I'd felt sure I'd made headway on disappeared. Snatched away without warning. The air became thick and syrupy. My footsteps became uncertain. I'd stumble and fall. Letters refused to come together on the page. How do you spell *jasmine*? What was my main character's name? I wouldn't be able to find certain letters on the keyboard. Sounds came to me as though I was submerged underwater. Was that my son babbling or the gurgling of blood rushing through my veins? For several hours, for a day or two, I'd be right back to square one, almost as broken as when I'd left the hospital.

Whenever I found myself giving up, giving in, I'd grab ahold of my son and take in the sweet scent of his baby skin and gaze into the dark gray of those knowing eyes. Like that, the decision to heal wasn't made in a single moment. I made the decision over and over and over again.

Then I made it one more time.

# 69

"The moment I saw my son being born," Scott has often said to me over the years, "I, too, was born as a father." A base animal instinct instantly awoke in him, needing to protect and nurture his son. *I'm your daddy*, he must have whispered possessively to Ishmael the first time he held his son close, every time he held his son close. Research shows that sometime between the second and fourth months, infants begin recognizing the faces of their primary caregivers. But did face recognition alone mean that Ishmael felt ties to his dad, even on a nonverbal level?

How tied did he now feel to me, given that I'd been absent from his life during these formative early months—and given, more importantly, that I was still struggling to bond with him? I was bathing my son in the kitchen sink. My mom was standing next to me, so close that our shoulders were bumping. It was the first time I'd bathed him on my own, and my mom was so afraid of me slipping up and hurting him that she had to keep her hands clasped behind her back just to prevent herself from interfering. My son was stretched out in a plastic baby bathtub, a look of contentment in his eyes. Now that he was four months old, he was babbling and blowing raspberries and clapping his hands. There was no doubt he recognized our faces and would hold my gaze for long seconds. My mom was talking to him as though they were in deep conversation, replying to his incessant babbling by saying things like, "You're right, you do have the cutest voice I've ever heard," and "You love having your mom bathe you, huh? Let's tell her to do it more often."

Chatting with my son didn't come naturally to me. The mother in me hadn't been born yet. Now that I was four months along in my recovery, I was still just recognizing him as my son. While my mom prattled on, I counted his ten fingers and his ten toes. I ran my hands up and down the length of his body, getting to know the contours of his muscles, the weight of his limbs. I lifted his chubby, bare legs in the air one at a time and kissed the soles of his feet. I carefully washed his sandy blond hair and cheeks, taking in his fragile wisps of eyebrows and lashes. I leaned over and blew raspberries onto his wet tummy. He screamed in delight, his laughter filling the house.

I thought that by doing those things mothers do, I might begin to feel like one too.

# 70

The Death Diet had reduced my weight to ninety-two pounds. When I look back on photos of this era, I catch myself peering closer at the images. Unable to immediately recognize myself, I wonder who that woman is holding my son. I am skeletal, my loam and flesh sucked dry. I recall that my continued weight loss frightened me into thinking that the disease hadn't left my body and I began pushing myself to set bigger and bigger goals. Quicker than anticipated, I built up the stamina and coordination to make my way from the back garden to the front door, then down the front steps, and then eventually down the block to the cul-de-sac. As thin as I was, the daily physical therapy routine I'd created for myself was strengthening my muscles. So by the time Ishmael's four-month well-baby appointment rolled around, I saw no reason not to accompany Scott. It was the first pediatric visit I'd attended and, not having met me before, the pediatrician asked if I was the nanny.

"Because my son is blond?" I asked, perceiving her comment as racist. My anger flared. My first thought was that I couldn't deal with any more racist doctors.

"Not at all," she immediately corrected me. Laughing to defuse the tension, she added, "Because you're so thin!"

Having grown accustomed to my intense emotions, Scott quickly took my hand into his and massaged it while he summarized my pregnancy complications to the doctor. I listened to her express her genuine sympathies before she asked how I was managing to care for my son. When I told her that my mom did the bulk of the caregiving, she made a remark in jest, nothing more than a quip, and yet it stayed with me.

"Too bad Grandma's not at today's appointment," she said. "She's probably best suited to answer my questions about Ishmael's development."

As we were leaving the appointment, I asked Scott if we could stop by the lactation center and rent a breast pump. The moment we got home, I retreated to the bedroom and latched the device to my body. The suction was much stronger than my son's natural rhythms, and I yelped in pain. Had it not been for the pediatrician's quip, I would have instructed Scott to return the pump that very afternoon and get our money back. Instead, I incorporated the pumping into my routine, strapping it on every four hours—even through the night. For the first time, it hit me how exhausting it was to be a new mother.

Nevertheless, I found myself refusing my mom's help. There had been a period of weeks early on when I'd considered Ishmael a threat to my survival, when I'd resented him for gobbling up my mom's attention when I needed her most. But something about the pediatrician's remark now made me start resenting my mom for gobbling up Ishmael's attention. He recognized her face, I knew that. But, when he looked at her, did he mistakenly think *she* was his mom? I was irrational, fueled on emotion because my thoughts were still murky. I began behaving in childish, hurtful ways that my mom didn't deserve. I'd walk out of a room with my son when she came in, bat away her hand even when it was clear I was struggling to get his diaper on, even shout at her to stop advising me on how to soothe him when he was throwing a fit. The same evening of his four-month well-baby appointment, I moved Ishmael out of my mom's bed and into a bassinet next to me.

# 71

I didn't sit my mom down and explain that it was time for her to go. I instead went behind her back to my dad. It had been two weeks since the pediatric appointment. It took that long for me to devise a plan. I knew that if I went to my mom directly, I'd both hurt her feelings and alarm her. The pediatrician was right. Not only was my mom most equipped to document Ishmael's development, but she was also most equipped to document mine. No doubt she would insist on staying, pointing out the ways I was still not capable of caring for my son on my own. Although my motor skills were returning quickly, there were other lingering deficits: twice in the past month my right eye had gone temporarily blind, shrinking my world, grinding me to a halt with a new kind of terror. Just as I was overcoming impairments and sensing a wider freedom of movement, there was something about losing my vision that trapped me right back inside my broken body. My judgment was also faulty—the reason I'd been mistreating my mom over the past two weeks, and the reason

I was now scheming to eject her from my home. Since my dad was in Minneapolis, he didn't have the close eye on me that she did and so, I calculated, he wouldn't know better than to go along with my plan.

When my mom was praying in her room, I called him and asked that he speak to my mom, tell her that it was time for her to come home.

"Just tell her you miss her," I suggested.

He laughed. He sounded relieved. He said, "I've been waiting a long time to get this call. Wanting your independence is a good sign that you're getting well. *Alhamdulillah*."

Short hours later, while my mom was hanging over me as I changed Ishmael out of his soiled clothes, my dad phoned her. Every instinct in me went alert. Rather than leave the room to take the call in private, my mom remained glued to me as she answered. Minutes into their conversation, she took a sharp breath, like I'd heard her take years ago when she was holding the light green aerogram in her hands, so I knew how much his words had shocked her. She glanced at me and lowered her voice, still unwilling to trust me enough to leave me alone with my son.

"Did she ask you to tell me to come home?" she said.

"Of course not!" I heard my dad say through the receiver, not betraying me. After a moment, he added, "It's been close to five months! You need to let her grow up."

When my mom continued to protest, he told her he'd give her five days to wrap everything up and say her goodbyes.

## 72

The closet where she'd stored her *shalwar kameez* was now mostly empty. Only the few items of clothing I'd purchased for my son when I was pregnant, items I no longer recognized, hung from the rod alongside empty hangers. My mom neatly folded my prayer rug, which she'd been using during her stay, and placed it respectfully on top of the dresser. Her suitcase was packed and ready to go. Even as I was taking all this in, I was thinking of how it must all be changed. Ishmael's crib had to be brought back up from the garage. The bed my mom had been using had to be stored away. The closet had to be filled with new clothes.

As I strapped Ishmael into his car seat, I could hear Scott grumbling as he loaded up the trunk with her bags. He was as against her leaving as my mom was, and we'd been arguing about it for several days. But even he knew better than to go up against my dad, not when my dad had finally accepted him into the family. I'd anticipated as much, which was another reason I'd turned to my dad for help. Scott would have had no trouble squashing the idea if it came from me. On the drive to the airport, I let my mom sit in the back seat next to Ishmael, enjoying her last minutes with him. Every few seconds, I heard a loud, wet sound as she kissed his hands, his feet, his cheeks.

Near the entrance to the security line, where the four of us paused to bid her farewell, my mom turned to me. She cleared her throat and held my gaze, so I knew she wanted me to listen carefully to what she was about to tell me. Having spent nearly five months living with her, even Scott recognized my mom's gesture and offered to take Ishmael on a quick stroll to give us some privacy.

"I know you're angry with God," my mom said the moment we were alone. "All these months, I've been using your prayer rug. I've been telling myself that I'm praying for the both of us until you're healed enough to pray yourself. But I'm scared you may never pray again." She took my hand into hers for a fleeting moment before letting it go. "Look," she said, gesturing to the crowded airport. All around us people were also saying their goodbyes. Just a few steps away, a couple was in the midst of a passionate kiss. Other grandparents were tightly embracing their grandchildren. There was a weighty sadness to the air that my senses narrowed in on.

"Can you remember what the word *kafir* means?" she asked.

I groaned and turned away. I wasn't in the mood for one of her religious lessons. I had gone from being angry at God to ignoring God, like a teen ghosting a former friend. Why couldn't she just tell me that she believed in me, that she knew I wouldn't harm my son, not even accidentally, and let it go at that?

She grabbed my chin and forced me to look at her. "Tell me what *kafir* means," she said.

*Kafir* was a word, like *qalam*, pen, that was the same in both Urdu and Arabic, spelled from right to left in the shared alphabet: kaaf, alif, faa, raa كافر. "Unbeliever," I told her.

She nodded her approval just like my Arabic tutor might have. Then, using the tone I hadn't heard in years, the one she often used when I was a child, she asked, "Is a *kafir* someone who doesn't believe in God?" She winked at me before adding, "Like your husband?"

I shook my head no. How many times had I learned this growing up? How often had I been made to understand the nuances of this definition when studying the Qur'an? A true unbeliever is not someone who doesn't believe in God; rather, a true unbeliever in the eyes of God is someone who is ungrateful.

I knew I would disappoint her, but I said it anyway: "I'm just not there yet. I'm sorry."

"Our saying goodbye at the airport might seem ordinary to you," she persisted just as Scott returned with Ishmael, "but I see a *mojiza*."

She ignored my shrug and took Ishmael in her arms a last time and hugged him so tightly he screamed and batted at her face. She bit his fingers and informed him in a high-pitched voice that she was taking pieces of him home with her. She thanked Scott for his hospitality. He thanked her for all her help, confessing that he wished she didn't have to leave. When she at last turned to say goodbye to me, she did what she always did when we said farewell, the only occasions when she let herself touch me. She cupped my face in both her hands and brought it close to hers, first kissing my right cheek and then my left cheek and then my forehead.

# 73

Buddhist monastics are trained to remain free of day-to-day entanglements by preparing for death. In the old Buddhist tradition, after years of meditation practice, monks would display their acceptance of death by splashing themselves with oil and lighting a match. If you were truly free of this world, you would be able to continue sitting in meditation, your concentration unwavering as your flesh went up in flames.

In Hinduism, a state of intense concentration has long been regarded as the highest stage of enlightenment one can achieve while still being bound to the body. It's when the consciousness of the self evaporates and the ultimate union with the divine is reached.

Samadhi, in Buddhism and Hinduism. Enlightenment, we say in English. Fana, according to Islam.

Some modest approximation of this state was what I'd always hoped to achieve in prayer and in meditation. But the internal chatter in my brain, its inability to stand still in time, had always tripped me up. Only when I was in the midst of writing, caught up in a flow, had I ever felt myself disappear.

Now that my mom was gone, the house felt unusually quiet. Bollywood movies were no longer running. Her constant chatter on the phone with my dad, my brothers, her friends, with my son and me—all that talking suddenly evaporated. The first morning I was alone with my son, just the two of us in the house while Scott was teaching, I walked from room to room. I ran my fingers across my mother-in-law's paintings. I stared at the many colorful book spines in the many bookshelves. Through the front windows, I watched the fog blowing down Twin Peaks and over rooftops and through redwood branches. I listened to a blue jay chirping in our garden, hidden from view among the lavender.

Time had gone still inside of me, but it didn't frighten me right then. Nor did the silence in my head. My breath slowed. Without the onslaught of stimulation that usually filled my home, distracting me, I was fully in the present moment. Each new second was pregnant with potential. Each second was endless. I started a new rhythm that day: I worked on my novel when my son napped. When he was awake, I turned that same intense concentration toward raising him.

# 74

Within a week of regular pumping, my body began producing milk. I was overjoyed. I felt like I'd overcome another kind of deficit. To celebrate, I dug out all the formula containers and all the plastic milk bottles from the kitchen cupboards and tossed them into the garbage.

The confidence I felt infused me with the courage to strap my son to my chest in a BabyBjörn and walk carefully down the block to the cul-de-sac before quickly retreating to the house again. It was the farthest I'd gone with my son without supervision, and I was both scared to be on my own but also exhilarated. My world had been the windowless, cramped cubicle of the neuro-ICU, subdued and dim. Then my world had been the four walls of my house. Now my world was this: the blowing fog, laughter from other pedestrians rushing by, the singing of birds in the trees overhead. Miles and miles of sky.

As the days went by and I grew even more sure of my abilities, I began taking longer and longer walks through the neighborhood. I couldn't help but feel powerful. In spite of my slim frame, I was winding my way up through narrow, steep streets and old, hidden staircases. Every day, I was getting closer and closer to making it to the summit of Twin Peaks. Not only that, but my muscles had become strong enough to carry my five-month-old strapped to my chest! I couldn't help but smile wildly at everyone I passed, wanting to shout my accomplishments at strangers even as I knew from their expressions and quickening gait that I was making them uncomfortable.

Days went on like this until one morning, just as I was exiting my house for another long walk, a neighbor simultaneously stepped out of her house with a small dog.

Look at that, I thought, watching her make her way down her front stoop with her dog on a leash. She's out walking a dog at the same time as I'm out walking my dog.

Just like that, in an instant, a wire came loose. In my mind, my son was no longer my son. My son was a dog. A small dog just like my neighbor's. She was out walking a dog. I was out walking a dog. She was headed toward me with her dog. I was headed toward her with my dog. That her dog was on a leash while mine was strapped to my chest was confusing. My mind struggled briefly, wondering why my dog was strapped to my chest, before discarding the discrepancy. We were both out walking our dogs!

As we drew nearer to each other, my neighbor glanced up at me and smiled. I waved. Her dog was digging at the root of a tree, then lifting a leg to pee. I wondered if my dog needed to pee too.

"You don't have a dog," I clearly heard a voice in my head say. It was calm and confident.

Yes, I do, I argued back.

"You don't have a dog," the voice said again with the same composure as before.

I quickly grew frustrated. The neighbor was a mere ten feet away. She was saying something to me. But I couldn't make out the words. I was in the midst of arguing with myself.

If I don't have a dog, then what do I have? I demanded. What am I out walking? I was genuinely struggling to understand what I had if not a dog. I genuinely wanted to know. But this other part of my brain refused to tell me.

"You don't have a dog," the voice simply repeated.

Right then, I came upon my neighbor. At the sight of me, her dog barked. The sound of the barking ignited the auditory systems in my brain and, just like that, zip, zip, zip, the information flashed like electricity through my neural pathways, and I was back on track.

I was out walking with my son.

It was the first mistake I'd made in the three weeks since my mom had left. I didn't think to turn back to the house. I was too alarmed. That evening, however, when Scott returned from teaching, I told him it might be a good idea to hire a part-time nanny.

# 75

The further along I got in my healing, the harder it was for me to endure the setbacks. When you're dealing with your feet and your hands and your eyes and your speech, the deficits are obvious. This made it easier for me to see what I was dealing with. Now that my deficits were largely in my higher processes of thinking and reasoning, my faulty cognition wasn't visible. It slipped right by me. I didn't realize I'd made a mistake until it was too late.

By the time my son's six-month well-baby appointment arrived, we'd hired a nanny for several hours a day. One afternoon while she was there, I decided that I would take my son to his checkup entirely on my own. Scott had missed too many classes as it was and, to make up for his absences, he'd been staying later and later at the university, meeting with students individually. He'd also been attending department meetings and reengaging with his colleagues to show his commitment to the program. Given everything on his plate, I saw no reason for him to miss another day of classes just to take Ishmael to a routine exam, especially, I reasoned, when I was capable of doing it myself.

So, I grabbed the car keys and told the nanny to strap Ishmael into his car seat. She hesitated for a second. Still hyper aware of emotions, I zeroed in on exactly what was going through her mind. She was worried I was going to harm my son. My anger quickly rose. *Why couldn't people just trust me?* I repeated myself more firmly.

"Strap Ishmael into his car seat, please."

She was new and didn't have the courage yet to go against me. After she strapped my son into his car seat, I reversed the car out of the driveway. I was not able to accurately gauge the distance between my car's rear end and the neighbor's car parked on the street and, before I knew what was happening, I smashed right into the neighbor's driver's-side door. I heard the glass of my rear brake lights smashing apart. I heard the crunching of steel. But I didn't think to stop. I didn't get out of the car. Somehow, crashing into another car seemed perfectly acceptable, a normal part of driving. The nanny began yelling and waving at me from the driveway, trying to get me to pull over. She was being hysterical for no reason. Ignoring her, I shifted the car into drive and jerked forward into the street. After several yards, I clipped the side mirror of another neighbor's car. Ishmael began crying, startled by all the noise and jostling. I sensed his fear. Instantly, some protective instinct in me was aroused. I'd let nothing harm my son!

I stopped the car. Through the rearview mirror, I saw the nanny racing toward us, horrified. She wrenched my son from the car seat. I, too, got out and, leaving the car in the middle of the road, I strolled back inside the house, trailing my son. The car remained in the middle of the street for the rest of the day, blocking traffic, until Scott rushed home early from teaching, panicked by what I'd done, and pulled it back into the garage. I watched him from the front windows as he went from one neighbor's house to the next and apologized. All I could think was that my maternal instincts had finally been born! At the sounds of my son's crying, I'd done exactly what I needed in order to protect him.

## 76

In the days following the car accident, I kept myself busy in the house. The realization that I could have harmed my son was slowly taking shape in my mind and I kept hearing his frightened cry. One afternoon, after I put Ishmael down for a nap in his crib, I found myself behaving in the kind of irrational fashion that my mom sometimes did. My concern for my son's safety reminded me of learning that he'd stopped breathing soon after birth and I suddenly became too paranoid to leave his side. To keep busy, I quietly cleared out his closet of items he'd outgrown while staying mindful of his slow, steady breath in and out. I was sitting on the floor packing up a pile of giveaways when I came upon a box shoved against the back wall, tucked behind the overnight bag I'd taken to the hospital. I opened the box to find baby gifts we'd received while I'd been recovering and my mom was staying in this room. Delighted, I dug through it, hanging up items of clothing he would grow into—a cute blue striped pullover, a flannel button-down that looked like a miniature version of what Scott might wear, soft brown leather shoes, a green baby blanket with a hedgehog stitched into a corner. I was sad to find tops and bottoms that were now too small for him still sitting in the box with tags attached. I added these to the growing pile of donations, which included the cute cotton one-piece with covered feet, printed with black-and-gold-striped zebras that I'd long ago intended to bring him home in. At the bottom of the box, I came upon a scrapbook with a bright red-and-blue cover. "BABY'S 1ST YEAR!" it declared in all caps across the front. The design was tacky, something I would never buy. It made sense that Scott had stored it away. And yet I held it in my hands like lost treasure. I ran my hand over the cover, tracing the letters with my finger, then flipped it open to the first page. The author had provided prompts then designed circles and squares for the answers. Baby's Name. Baby's Date of Birth. Baby's Time of Birth. Baby's Birth Weight. Baby's Apgar Score. A space to tape Baby's Footprint and another space to tape Baby's Handprint. There was even a place to tape a lock of Baby's Hair.

I raced to my desk and found a pen in a drawer. I then raced back to the nursery and sat in the rocking chair with the scrapbook on my lap. I opened it again to the first page. I hadn't written with a pen in months, not since before the delivery—but even then it was merely to sign hospital paperwork. I fumbled with the pen for a moment, trying to remember exactly how to hold it correctly. When it felt like I'd gotten a good handle, in the space provided for Baby's Name, I carefully began to write my son's name, letter by letter, from left to right: I, S, H, M, A, E, L. My hand trembled as I wrote.

I forced myself to concentrate. I didn't want to misspell his name. The last time I'd paid such close attention to my son's name was back when I was pregnant and Scott and I had compiled a list of potential names. I had been inspired then by Hagar's story of faith, but now I saw only the hardships in that narrative, the cruel abandonment of her and her child, the isolation, the unsteady repetition of her footsteps in the hot desert sand as she stumbled back and forth between two hills, searching for salvation.

When I was done writing my son's name, I scrutinized my penmanship. My handwriting was messy, the letters uneven. I felt embarrassed. I'd written my son's name in all caps: ISHMAEL. Had my brain somehow copied the format of the title, taking it as a guideline? It was a stark reminder of where I was at in my development. I wished I'd used a pencil so I could erase and start over. Below his name were other prompts that I now read over: date of birth, time of birth, birth weight, Apgar score. I didn't know the answers. I'd have to wait for Scott to get home and ask his help. Not wanting to miss further milestones, I flipped through the pages to see what I should be on the lookout for: Baby's 1st Tooth. Baby's 1st Word. Baby's 1st Step. The scrapbook was like a blueprint guiding me through motherhood. The comfort I took from this was short-lived. When Ishmael woke from his nap and I was nursing him on the rocking chair, I noticed his first tooth had already come in. When did that happen? It was a sign that I'd missed more than I would ever realize. The sorrow I felt wasn't new anymore. Pain and loss were like the dark spots in my brain marking this era of my life.

That evening, I sat with Scott on the sofa and we filled in the first few pages of the scrapbook together. I wrote down the answers based on Scott's memory. He teased that my penmanship was as illegible as the doctors' notes in the discharge papers. I joked that a professor's was no better. Near our feet, Ishmael was lying on top of the green fleece blanket with the hedgehog stitched in the corner, a gift sent to me by someone whose name I didn't recognize, someone whose memory had burned away. Something about my son's erratic movements caught my eye and I stopped writing. Putting the book and pen down, I lowered myself to the floor to sit beside Ishmael. While on his belly, he was jerking his arms and legs, as though he were trying to swim across the room. I picked him up and held him upright. He automatically pointed his feet like a ballerina and tried to stand on his toes.

"*Chulte?*" I said in Urdu, asking if he wanted to walk.

While I held him upright, he stood on tiptoes with knees locked then suddenly unlocked his knees and crumpled under his own weight, then, just as swiftly, locked them into place and stood bowlegged again.

Scott watched us with a bemused smile before saying, "Why are you tormenting him? He can't walk yet."

"I know," I said quietly, and I meant it in a way Scott couldn't possibly understand. I knew with all my being that my son couldn't possibly walk yet. I knew how complicated the process of walking actually was, and how the body and the brain had to work perfectly in concert for him to make the smallest of steps. But I also could see the development taking place, the nascent messages being sent by electrical impulses, directing his arms and legs to move like a little swimmer on the floor, every instinct in him driving him forward. I may have lost meaningful milestones over the past year, but I knew I'd gained an insider's knowledge into what was coming ahead.

# 77

For one of my routine follow-up visits, I'd been scheduled by chance to see the same neurologist who'd been at my side every moment I was in the neuro-ICU. The exam room was located on the seventh-floor neurology ward, eight floors below where I delivered my son and down the hallway from the double doors to the neuro-ICU. I had to walk past those heavy locked doors to get to where I needed to be. It was an ordinary exam room, no different from the many others I'd sat in alone or with Scott over the past three and a half years since delivery. With the softness of tone that I remembered so well, the neurologist conducted the usual neuro-assessment, checking my reflexes, shining a light into my pupils, having me push and pull on his hands, walking in a straight line. Afterward, he asked me to hop down from the exam table and take a seat in the plastic chair. He pulled out a black-and-white image of my brain from that morning's MRI scan and held it up against a white screen for me to see, pointing out dark areas at several points along the tissue.

"These are the leftover stains from the injury," he explained. "These aren't going to go away. Think of them as your brain's personal signature now."

I nodded. I wasn't that invested in what he was saying. The news was always the same, no matter how much time elapsed. There was still more healing for me to do.

Seeing that I was mistaking what he was trying to tell me, he smiled and added, "By leftover stains, I mean these are now considered old injuries."

Then he gave me the news I'd been waiting so long to hear; news I feared I would never hear. He told me the reason he wanted to show me the imaging was because my scans had all come back normal, my brain beautifully deflated and terrifically wrinkled, the old injuries visually apparent like dark bruises were now simply a part of who I was. The darkness and the light.

Even as the neurologist said the words *recover* and *heal*, however, he reminded me he was using these words hesitantly. "You might always have to deal with some level of mild aphasia," he said, "and I know you are still occasionally experiencing difficulties with your memory." He took a seat in his upholstered chair and pulled open a desk drawer. "See how everything inside is shaking from the movement?" he said, referring to the pens and containers of hand sanitizers. "Think of your neural connections like that. The movement is good. The movement means there's still improvements to come." He closed the drawer and rolled his chair toward me. "From a medical standpoint, you've healed better than I anticipated. Some of those pieces are going to keep adjusting and sorting themselves out, but this is it. No need for any more follow-up exams."

I must have looked as stunned as when I'd first woken up in the neuro-ICU and found myself staring at him. After all my efforts to regain my English fluency, all words now left me. I could do nothing but smile. I smiled wide and I smiled hard and I kept on smiling even as I wept. I sensed how deeply gratifying this moment was for him too. He was a doctor who'd devoted his life to caring for patients who have the misfortune of landing behind those double doors. He confided that in his twenty-plus-year career as a neurologist, he was able to count on one hand the number of patients who'd been able to overcome their deficits. And of those he could count on one hand, I was the only one to have endured such scope and magnitude of injuries. He'd never witnessed anyone go as far as I had gone and make it back.

"How did you do it?" he asked, unable to hide his curiosity.

I didn't have an answer for him. So I found myself saying what he himself told me long ago. "I can't take credit for my recovery."

"But what have you been doing?" he pressed. "I'm a doctor. I can only assess what I see from the outside. Tell me what you did from the inside."

"I wrote a book," I blurted, not knowing what else to say.

The idea intrigued him and we delved into the topic for some time, exploring different aspects and possibilities. He hypothesized that the repetitive process of working on a story based on my personal experience forced my brain to excavate my past, stimulating my memory in ways it wouldn't have been otherwise. I was forcing my brain to think back on my life, to call up experiences and emotions, to remember what it was like being back in the dusty alleys in the Old City of Hyderabad, to smell the heat and taste the spices of those streets and to hear the call to prayer filling the sky from loudspeakers. Writing forced me to take those memories and emotions and senses and distill them into a scene, to animate different characters, each with a mind of his or her own, into dialogue and conflicting motives and then to project a future trajectory for each one. To hold the authority of the narrator. To be a presence at every step without calling attention to my presence. It forced me to plan and plot, to be strategic about the various possible consequences of the unfolding events. And to correctly match the words I was typing with those springing to mind. In this way, for months and then for years, each day I sat down at the computer, I pushed my brain to create new connections.

While I'd sensed it before, it was clear to me now, from this conversation, that so much of my life had depended upon me writing the book. As brain damaged as I'd been, some small part of me—or perhaps something much larger than me—understood that my global trauma required this global treatment.

# 78

I couldn't think of anyone I wanted to celebrate the good news with more than my son. So I began walking down the steep Parnassus Heights hill and across the valley to his preschool with the intention of picking him up early. As I walked away from the hospital and toward my son, I couldn't help but feel like I was finally making my way out of the desert.

At the sight of me, my son's face lit up and he dropped the toys he was holding and instantly ran over and hugged me. As excited as he was to see me, I could tell his brain didn't register time yet. He didn't understand that it was a little past noon, that he'd only been at preschool for half the normal day. As we left together, the teachers wished him farewell but it didn't occur to him to reply. At three-and-a-half years old, his brain was still making synaptic connections. He was learning to speak fluently in English, learning to write. He was just beginning to discern social cues. His social environment was literally shaping his brain. But it was a long process, and he still had a lengthy adventure ahead of him.

"Say bye to your teachers," I reminded him as we left.

He gave a half-hearted wave and rushed out of the front door. I swung his Buzz Lightyear backpack over my shoulder and we began walking home. I didn't say anything. It'd been a long time since my mind was utterly blank. No chatter whatsoever. Words were crushed under the weight of emotions. For years, I'd anticipated that once the neurologist pronounced me normal I would feel victorious, even arrogant. But I didn't feel anything like that. I was in wonder. I felt like my parents must have when watching *The Ten Commandments* and witnessing God's miracles.

As I walked alongside my son, I sensed a magical quality to everything around me. The branches of the redwood trees, the expansiveness of the sky, even the asphalt road sparkled with beauty. My son noticed it too, and he frequently stopped on the way home, stooping to admire every pebble he encountered, passing his hand over every leaf of every bush lining the sidewalk, gazing at every slug bug, and I crouched down next to his small body, in wonder myself. What an enchanting world. Every crack and fissure on every slab of cement along every sidewalk was cleanly delineated. Every vein on a leaf pulsed with life. The feel of the soft velvet of a rose petal between my fingers sent giggles of joy through us. My son and I passed objects between us, sharing what we found like treasure, enraptured.

Look at the various hues of gray on that river rock. Look at the sharpness of this blade of grass. We examined every trunk of every tree we passed, grazing our palms over the whorls of knots, the jagged layers of bark. The brownest brown I'd ever beheld. The greenest of greens. There was no end to life's wonder.

# Epilogue

My daughter's name is Zaara.

When I was pregnant and my husband and I were researching the name, we discovered its many spellings, depending on the language you speak. *Zarah* in Swahili, while the Hindi variation changes slightly in spelling and pronunciation, *Sarita*. In Sicily, there's a theory that the name might be rooted in the orange tree flower, *zagara*, or in the early inhabitants of the city of Zadar on the Dalmatian coast, and the Venetian version becomes Zadra. In many parts of Spain, the letter *z* is pronounced not with a hard *zzz* sound but a softer *th*, so for them my daughter's name sounds like *Thara*. In Bulgarian, the name changes to *Zaharina*. If you live in Pakistan, you will say *Zahra*. The malleability of the name, its universality, is what drew us to it. More commonly spelled Zara with one *a*, the name has its roots in both Arabic and Hebrew. While the name means *princess* in Hebrew, it has multiple meanings in Arabic, including *radiance, flower, shining, bright*. Zaara is a variation of the Biblical Sarah and

Qur'anic Sara, the matriarch who, in all three Abrahamic scriptures, was the wife of the prophet Abraham and the mother to Isaac—the half-brother of Ishmael. As a feminine form of Zechariah, from a religious standpoint, Zaara means *God remembers*.

Eight years after my son was born, with the same ease as it occurred the first time around, I got pregnant with my daughter. In the years since I visited my neurologist for what became my final follow-up exam, I hadn't been back to the UCSF-Stanford Hospital up on the Parnassus Street hill. The hospital had since changed its name and was now simply called UCSF. But the pilgrimage up the hill started up once more, this time with my new husband.

Five years earlier, the same night of my last neurological exam, when Scott arrived home from teaching, I'd told him the good news. I recalled every word the doctor asked me to remember and repeat back to him. I could see perfectly how many fingers the doctor was holding up, no matter where in my field of vision he was holding them up. When he asked me to reach out and touch his finger, I was able to find it. I spread my arms wide open and touched my own nose. I walked in a straight line. I even hopped on one leg! Scott listened with a warm smile on his face, not once interrupting. When I was done reporting everything I could remember, I went back to the beginning and reported it a second time. He hugged me. We celebrated.

By creating new neural pathways my brain didn't do anything special. Our brains are flexible enough to continuously build new circuits. It's exactly what a newborn's brain does as it develops, exactly what my son's newborn brain began doing from the moment he was born. He and I just happened to build new circuits at about the same time. My brother had hoped this would happen when he spoke to me on the day of my discharge about using my newborn as my inspiration. What my brother didn't tell me was that just as my son's brain was forming to create a wholly unique individual in Ishmael, I, too, was reengineering myself down to my very wiring, transforming into an entirely new person. I had no choice. Giving birth to my son, it turned out, required that I bury my old self. It was one of the most difficult challenges I faced during the healing process. How do you say goodbye to the person you remember yourself to be? How do you accept that everything you are, your perceptions of the world and your physical abilities and your likes and dislikes and your memories of your past and your attachments to others are nothing more than the soft white substance of your brain?

That night of my last neurology exam, I helped my son through his bedtime rituals. Because I'd taken him out of preschool early, we'd spent the entire afternoon together, walking up hidden staircases and steep hills that I'd once carried him up in my BabyBjörn. He was three years old and exhausted, his little legs aching from our long hours of roaming the curvy, narrow streets. While he soaked in a hot bathtub, playing with a blue plastic orca, I shampooed his silky hair, which had slowly darkened over the years to a light brown. I soaped up his tummy and back. Then I grabbed the toy orca from his hands and sprayed water on him from a hole in its mouth. He screamed in delight. When his eyes became heavy with sleep, I wrapped his small body in a towel and helped him to slide his growing arms and legs into his favorite dinosaur pajamas. While he stood on a step stool in front of the bathroom mirror, I guided the toothbrush into his mouth, my hand clasped gently over his as we brushed his teeth together. Then I sat him on the toilet, standing right beside him, as he did his business for the last time of the day before getting into bed. *There will come a time when he can do this by himself*, I thought all the while, watching his little form. *There will come a time when he doesn't need me anymore.* Watching him grow and change and become more independent was bittersweet. We were bonded by ties that went beyond maternal love. I'd become so attached to him that I was aware of every ebb and flow of our bond, every move he made toward me, every step away.

The next morning, Scott and I got down to the business of doing what we'd been discussing for a while. Now that I was well, we started to plan our separation. After three and a half years, we were no longer bonded to each other by love, but by trauma. I was no longer the young woman who gleefully married him right after graduation from the writing program. After having spent my childhood years trying to become the person my parents expected me to be, I couldn't now try to become the woman Scott remembered. He was depleted from caring for me and eager for a fresh start at a new life. Now that I could envision a future, I was excited to step into it.

Back at the same hospital where I had delivered my son, back in this OB exam room that I remembered so well, my new husband now sat next to me. While he was ethnically

Indian like me, he'd been born and raised in the U.S. and our one common language was English. He was taller and wider than Scott and looked terribly uncomfortable in the plastic chair. There had been no grand Indian wedding for us with celebrations lasting over five days. Nor had we held a small private ceremony in his parents' back garden in San Jose. We'd both been married before. We both had sons from our first marriages who were close in age. We were both older this time around, in our late thirties. When we married, we'd secretly eloped to Napa.

Now that I was pregnant, I'd come back to the same hospital because it was the only local hospital to know my history, and so, as ironic as it seemed, the only one that could keep me safe. This time, I entrusted my care to a female obstetrician, who promised to listen to my concerns. And she did. We knew the risks. If it happened again, if my body exploded a second time around, there would be no putting me back together. I was older now. The neuroplasticity wasn't as fluid. And my body had already suffered from severe trauma. There would be no Miracle Girl because there would be nothing remaining of the girl. My story would come to an end.

All my previous doctors were put on alert, including my cardiologist, my nephrologist, and of course my neurologist. As it happened, my younger brother was now finishing his surgical residency here so he came with me to the appointments, knowing the right questions to ask. Because he always showed up in scrubs and made a point to tell my physicians of his own affiliation to the hospital, the doctors would open up and converse with him in their shared medicalese.

Together, as a team, they watched over me at each monthly appointment and also in between. Hearing I was pregnant, my parents began checking up on me every day, concerned about my well-being but elated to be grandparents again. My mom insisted on flying over to help, but I had no date to give her because I had no idea how this might play out. If the old symptoms started showing up again, my OB would immediately deliver the baby, no matter how prematurely.

I spent weeks terrified, as though a time bomb was ticking down inside me. I had lengthy chats on the phone with Naomi, who was now living in New Haven and teaching at Yale. In a moment of weakness, I once called my older brother in New York and asked if he thought I'd made a mistake wanting another baby. There was no ignoring this familiar sensation beating through my growing and expanding body. Just as I had awakened to the wonder of life, seeing it from innocent eyes, now I was seeing the world around me with the knowledge that it might be the last time. But my life didn't flash before my eyes. I didn't confront moments when I'd been errant. Nor did I envision handing God my Book of Deeds before crossing a bridge. Instead, I unfolded my prayer rug and touched my forehead to the ground in prayer. The reality that my clock might be ticking down expanded each day, each hour, each second, making it more magical than I thought possible, deeply precious.

There were nights when I couldn't sleep and lay next to my son in his bed. At nine years old, his long, lean body came up to my shoulders. His face was still changing and developing so that at times I caught glimpses of my dad's broad features in his while, at other times, he looked exactly like Scott. Although I thought I was doing a good job of shielding him from the risks of my pregnancy, one day when I picked him up from school, his fourth-grade teacher informed me that, every day in class that week, he'd been breaking down in tears, panicked that he was going to lose his mom. Even as I assured Ishmael that I was never going to leave him, I couldn't help but wonder during those sleepless nights, as I stared at his face, what would happen to him if I didn't make it. I'd made every effort to be a constant presence in his life, to not be relegated to a ghost inhabiting some edge of his existence, and yet here I was staring down at that same gloomy prospect again. It was to leave my son with some legacy that I began writing the first draft of this memoir, documenting what I might not get a chance to tell him myself.

In the end, I didn't make it to my due date. When the very first red flag popped up late in the third trimester, and my face and my fingers started bloating, and my daughter's heartbeat started slowing and weakening, my obstetrician stepped in immediately. She took the warning sign seriously. That very night, six weeks before my daughter's due date, she performed an emergency C-section, saving me before the disease overtook and destroyed my organs. Although I'd been warned that my baby girl would require a stay in the NICU and a steroid injection to jump-start her lungs, she defied the odds. She came out kicking and screaming, healthy and strong. She passed the Apgar test with flying colors. Minutes after her birth, the nurse bathed my daughter and wrapped her in a white cotton hospital blanket printed with the design of brightly colored baby footprints. I watched all this from across the room. When the nurse finally laid my newborn daughter in my arms, right across my chest, my husband, dressed in blue scrubs, began snapping photos.

Holding my daughter for the first time, I counted her ten fingers and her ten toes. I ran my hand through the softness of her thick, black hair. I was smitten. Minutes later, as I was still holding my daughter, breathing in her sweet newborn scent, I was wheeled into a recovery room that I recognized immediately. It was the same room on the maternity ward where Scott had stayed while I was in the neuro-ICU, the same room I'd been transferred to before being discharged from the hospital. The same minute I recognized the room, Scott seemed to miraculously appear before me. He'd come to drop off Ishmael, who was eager to meet his sister and more eager, it seemed, to see with his own eyes that I had made it through. It crossed my mind to tell him that he'd been in this very room as a newborn, but I thought better of it. Death and rebirth, the circular nature of time, ghosts, and hauntings. That I was back in this room was a sign, but one meant only for me. When Scott quickly took his leave, my husband went with him, saying he'd walk Scott to the elevators. But I knew what he was really doing. He wanted to give me a moment alone with my son.

The cesarean incision was fresh, a black thread running from left to right, right to left across my lower belly. My daughter was sleeping on my chest. Since the nurse had placed her in my arms, I hadn't been able to let her go. Holding her securely, I scooted over on the hospital bed, making room for my son to join. "Come meet your sister," I told him, reaching out to take his hand in mine. When my son had climbed in and was lying beside me with his arm protectively across his new sister and me, I noted how cozily we three fit together. A perfect little puzzle. "Zaara, this is your big brother," I said, introducing the two. "This is Ishmael."

# Acknowledgments

A memoir is an account of a pivotal time in a writer's life. But I don't have first-hand memories or the necessary medical knowledge to describe the most life-changing event I've ever endured. So I am grateful to those who generously filled in the holes in my story: my best friend, Naomi; my son's father and my ex-husband, T; and my two brothers.

Preeclampsia is a complicated pregnancy disorder that even the best brains in the world are trying to better understand. Dr. Susan Fisher granted me entrance into her lab at UC San Francisco, where she is the director of Translational Research in Perinatal Biology and Medicine. Whatever crucial knowledge I was able to impart in this book about the disease comes from her groundbreaking research. Preeclampsia is a leading cause of pregnancy-related death, and Dr. Fisher has devoted her life to saving others'. We women need more medical heroes like Dr. Fisher. One of the first OB/GYNs to publish on preeclampsia/HELLP syndrome, back in the 1970s, was Dr. Maurice L. Druzin at Stanford Medicine. Dr. Druzin's subspecialty is high-risk obstetrics, and he graciously took time away from his practice to share his extensive knowledge with me with the hopes that it might help to save even more lives. Dr. Patricia Robertson at UCSF courageously agreed to take on the heavy responsibility of safeguarding me through my second pregnancy. Dr. Robertson's own book, *The Premature Labor Handbook: Successfully Sustaining Your High-Risk Pregnancy*, published in 1985, was the first book to comprehensively address preterm labor and the related issues confronting women. I am proud to have an autographed copy in my private library. Dr. Wade Smith, my neurologist at UCSF, doesn't take credit for my recovery—so it seems only fitting that, while I thanked him in the acknowledgments of my novel for "helping to give me a second life," I thank him a second time here.

Dr. Smith might have been the first to suggest I write this memoir, but I can honestly say that it wouldn't have been published without my dream team. My über-talented literary agents at Janklow & Nesbit, Emma Parry and Julia Eagleton, were steadfast in their faith, encouragement, and support. I couldn't have asked for two smarter or savvier women in my corner. What a blessing you two have been. I am indebted to my editor, Kendall Storey, at Catapult, whose vision and massive talents helped to shape this narrative. How could I have been so lucky? And Megan Fishmann for being fire and also lighting a fire.

Finally, I want to thank my parents for not always understanding my life choices but nonetheless making the choice to stand by me. To my two children, who are the breath between my breath. I hope I've done you proud! This book would not have been written without the love and support of my husband, R, whose name in Sanskrit means "sun." True to his name, even in my darkest moments, especially in my darkest moments, R has been a steady, much-needed light in my life.

**SAMINA ALI** is the author of *Madras on Rainy Days*, which won the French Prix du Premier Roman Étranger and was a finalist for the PEN/ Hemingway Award in Fiction. She is also a recipient of a Rona Jaffe Foundation Writers' Award. Her writing has been featured in various outlets, from national NPR to *The Economist*.